HULI OF PAPUA
A Cognatic Descent System

ÉCOLE PRATIQUE DES HAUTES ÉTUDES - SORBONNE
VIe SECTION : SCIENCES ÉCONOMIQUES ET SOCIALES

CAHIERS DE L'HOMME
Ethnologie - Géographie - Linguistique

NOUVELLE SÉRIE VIII

PARIS   **MOUTON & CO**   THE HAGUE
MCMLXVIII

ROBERT M. GLASSE

HULI OF PAPUA
A Cognatic Descent System

WITH A FOREWORD
BY J. A. BARNES

PARIS   **MOUTON & CO**   THE HAGUE
MCMLXVIII

© *1968 by Mouton & Co, and École Pratique des Hautes Études.*
Printed in France

FOREWORD

At every stage in the history of anthropology there have been certain tribes or groups of peoples who have attracted more than local professional interest and whose social institutions have been studied for the light they seemed to throw on the processes underlying the growth of human society everywhere. For several decades during the nineteenth century the Australian Aborigines and the unfortunate Tasmanians enjoyed this special ethnographic status, while in the twenties and thirties of this century the inhabitants of the Trobriand Islands, in superb isolation from the rest of Melanesia, acquired worldwide renown through the spirited advocacy of Malinowski. Since mid-century the increased amount of ethnographic fieldwork and ethnological writing has prevented the emergence of any single group as the current fashionable prototypical tribe comparable to the Navaho and the Nuer of earlier years. But along with several other areas the Highlands of Papua and New Guinea has come to be recognized, even by anthropologists whose regional interests lie elsewhere, as the home of a group of societies that cannot be overlooked in any discussion of the general characteristics of human culture and social institutions. The broad similarities in environment, natural resources, technical development, mode of political and domestic life, length and content of Western contact and, presumably, in cultural history provide, as it were, laboratory conditions for the investigation of many significant variations on a common base. The task of understanding these variations is a long way from completion, but already it is clear that ideas derived from ethnographic and archaeological studies in other parts of the world about, for example, the nature of descent and filiation, the exclusiveness of social allegiance in tribal society, the relation of religious belief to everyday behaviour, and the antiquity of mature horticulture must be revised in the light of Highlands evidence.

One of the first anthropologists to recognize the importance of the study of Highland societies for a wider understanding of social life in general was the late Professor S. F. Nadel. Reports by several of those students who went to New Guinea under his aegis have become a substantial part of the ethnographic literature of the area. The present work by Dr. Glasse, a doctoral thesis presented at the Australian National University in 1962, stems directly from this original impetus, even though it was completed after Nadel's untimely death. Pressure of other commitments has delayed its publication but its appearance is very welcome. The Huli people, whose social arrangements for peace and war, marriage, residence and cultivation are described in this book, have hitherto been known only from two tantalizingly short journal articles published in 1959, a chapter in Lawrence and Meggitt's 1965 symposium on religion, *Gods, Ghosts and Men in Melanesia* (Melbourne, Oxford University Press) and microfilm copies of Dr. Glasse's thesis. Several commentators on the societies of the Highlands have seen the Huli as a controversial people, providing exceptions to some neat generalizations as well as corroborative evidence for some others. This is not the place for another appraisal of the morphological and historical relations of the Huli to other Highland societies, and the reader is referred to J. B. Watson's symposium, "Anthropology in the New Guinea Highlands" (1964, *American Anthropologist*, 66: 4,2) and Marie de Lepervanche's article "Descent, Residence and Leadership in the New Guinea Highlands" (1967-68, *Oceania*, 38: 134-158, 163-189). Rereading this thesis in the light of the arguments and counter-arguments that have been advanced during the six years that have elapsed since it was first submitted, I am confident that while Huli institutions are likely to remain analytically controversial, the wider dissemination of the evidence contained in the thesis will enable more readers to get closer to the facts about this most fascinating part of Melanesia, and closer to a firm understanding of the traditional way of life of the Highlanders who live there.

Dr. Glasse first visited the Huli only four years after an Australian administrative patrol post had been opened among them, and he was able to gather reliable information about customary and actual patterns of living essentially unaffected by colonial and missionary contact. Since that time major changes in social control, religious belief and practice, and economic life have affected the Huli along with most other Highland societies. No one who has been in the Highlands can doubt that these vigorous and confident people, keen to master the new world of opportunity that they see before them, will have new lessons to teach those who remain to study their adaptation to changed conditions. These lessons too may perhaps have a significance that will reach out beyond New Guinea. Meanwhile we have the task of understanding an earlier and most impressive cultural achievement, the intricate variations on a common theme displayed by the linked indigenous societies of the Highlands, and of relating this understanding to similar, and not-so-similar, groups of societies in other parts of the world.

Institute of Advanced Studies.
Australian National University.
April, 1968.

J. A. BARNES.

This study was presented as a thesis for the Ph.D. in Anthropology at the Australian National University in 1962. Owing to the pressure of other fieldwork, it has not been revised. I have judged it better to publish it in this form, than to take more time to re-write it and to relate the conclusions to studies of cognatic societies which have appeared since it was written.

The data presented here were gathered during two field trips: the first as a research student at the Australian National University, and the second as the Walter Mersh Strong Fellow at the University of Sydney. The initial period lasted from April 1955 until June 1956, the final period from June, 1959 until February, 1960—a total of about 22 months. I am grateful to both Universities for their generous support. I acknowledge also with gratitude the hospitality and pratical help I received from officers of the Papua and New Guinea Administration, especially from Mr. William Crellin, the Assistant District Officer at Tari during both periods. I am indebted also to the members of the Methodist Overseas Mission at Tari, headed by the Reverend Roland Barnes. I also thank Mr. and Mrs. W. M. Rule of the Unevangelized Fields Mission who kindly gave me a copy of their Huli grammar.

The thesis was written under the supervision of Professor J. A. Barnes. I am most grateful to him for his help and patient interest. I have also profited greatly from discussions with Professor W. R. Geddes and Doctors H. Ian Hogbin, J. D. Freeman, M. J. Meggitt and R. N. H. Bulmer.

Finally, my greatest debt is to the Huli people, who allowed me to live among them for so long and who patiently instructed me in their lore and learning.

Queens College
Flushing, New York.

R. M. G.

TABLE OF CONTENTS

Chapter I — INTRODUCTION 15
 Discovery; early contact; distribution of the population; country and climate; the people; the problem.

Chapter II — FUNDAMENTALS OF GROUP STRUCTURE 23
 Residence; descent affiliation of parish members; parish composition; Tunda parish, a detailed example; summary and discussion.

Chapter III — LAND TENURE 37
 Land resources; principles of land-holding; validating claims and transferring titles; Tunda land-holding.

Chapter IV — MARRIAGE AND THE FAMILY 47
 Marriage rates; marriage choices; initiating marriage; bride price; establishing a union; affinal relations; family and household composition; family residential patterns; dissolution of marriage by death; divorce; norms of marital experience.

Chapter V — COGNATIC DESCENT AND THE INDIVIDUAL 77
 Genealogy and the individual; mode of residence; agnation and cognation.

Chapter VI — CONFLICT 87
 Sources of conflict; murder and suicide; the conduct of war; organization of war; synopses of war histories; sorcery; poison; ritual cursing; ritual conflict.

Chapter VII — COMPENSATION 111
 Damages; preliminaries to war indemnity; wergild; case studies: case 1 – residence and responsibility; case 2 – the consequences of a seduction; descent and indemnity; summary and discussion.

Chapter VIII — COGNATIC SOCIETY 133

Appendices I to VI 143
   Acreage of Tunda gardens held by individuals in divided ownership, 1960. — Acreage held in full and residual titles by members of Tunda parish, 1960. — Extent of land-holding and parish membership. — Huli kin terms. — Relationship between mode of residence and age of Huli men. — A bride price conflict.

TABLES

1.	The Size and Population of Tari and Koroba Census Divisions, 1960	18
2.	The Adult Male Members of Five Parish Groups, 1959	27
3.	Analysis of Association between Residence and Mode of Affiliation.	30
4.	Men of Tunda Parish, by Section, 1959	32
5.	The Residents of Tunda Parish-Territory, by Section, 1959	33
6.	Comparison of Tunda Parish Members with and without Titles to Land on Tunda Parish-Territory	43
7A.	Descent and the Extent of Tunda Land-Holding	44
7B.	Residence and the Extent of Tunda Land-Holding	44
8.	Marital Status of Huli Men	47
9.	Contributors to Bride Price	56
10.	Recipients of 18 Bride Price Payments	58
11.	Huli Affinal Behaviour	60
12.	Residence of Huli Married Couples	65
13.	Residence of Adult Brothers	66
14.	Remarriage of Widows to Kinsmen of their Late Husbands and Other Men	69
15.	The Amount of Bride Price Paid for Widows by Kinsmen of the Late Husband and Unrelated Men	69
16.	The Ostensible Reasons why Husbands Initiate Divorce	72
17.	The Ostensible Reasons why Wives Divorce their Husbands	72

18.	Norms of Huli Marital Experience	74
19.	Number of Activated and Potential Parish Ties of 229 Men	80
20.	Exploitation of Cognatic Parish Ties by 229 Men	81
21.	Consensus and Individual Evaluations of Parish Membership	83
22.	Classification of Alleged Injuries of 119 Huli Men	88
23.	Some Characteristics of Huli Warfare	91
24.	Contributions to Huli Reparations	118
25.	Recipients of Reparations for Yulupe's Death	120
26.	Distribution of Reparations for the Death of Teabe's Wife	121
27.	Contributions to Huli Wergild Payments	123
28.	Contributions to Kaube's Wergild	126
29.	Analysis of Contributions to Wergild and Reparations	130
30.	Summary of Main Compensation Relationships	131

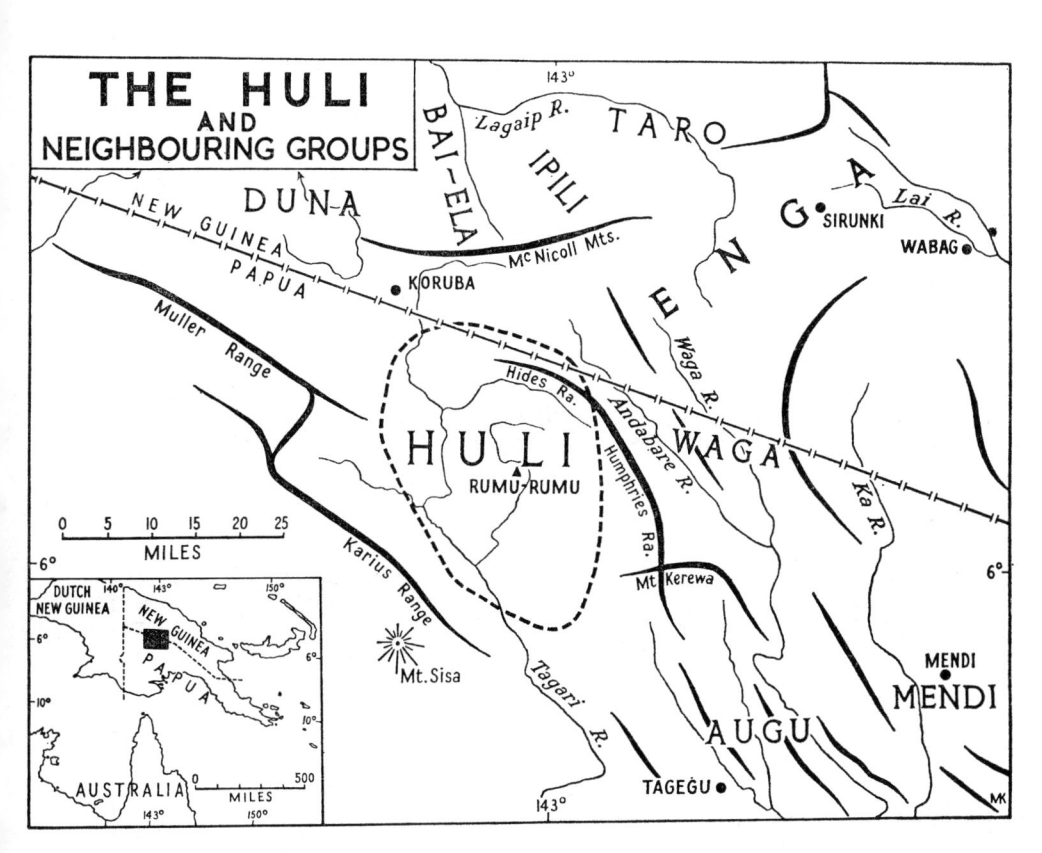

MAP 1.

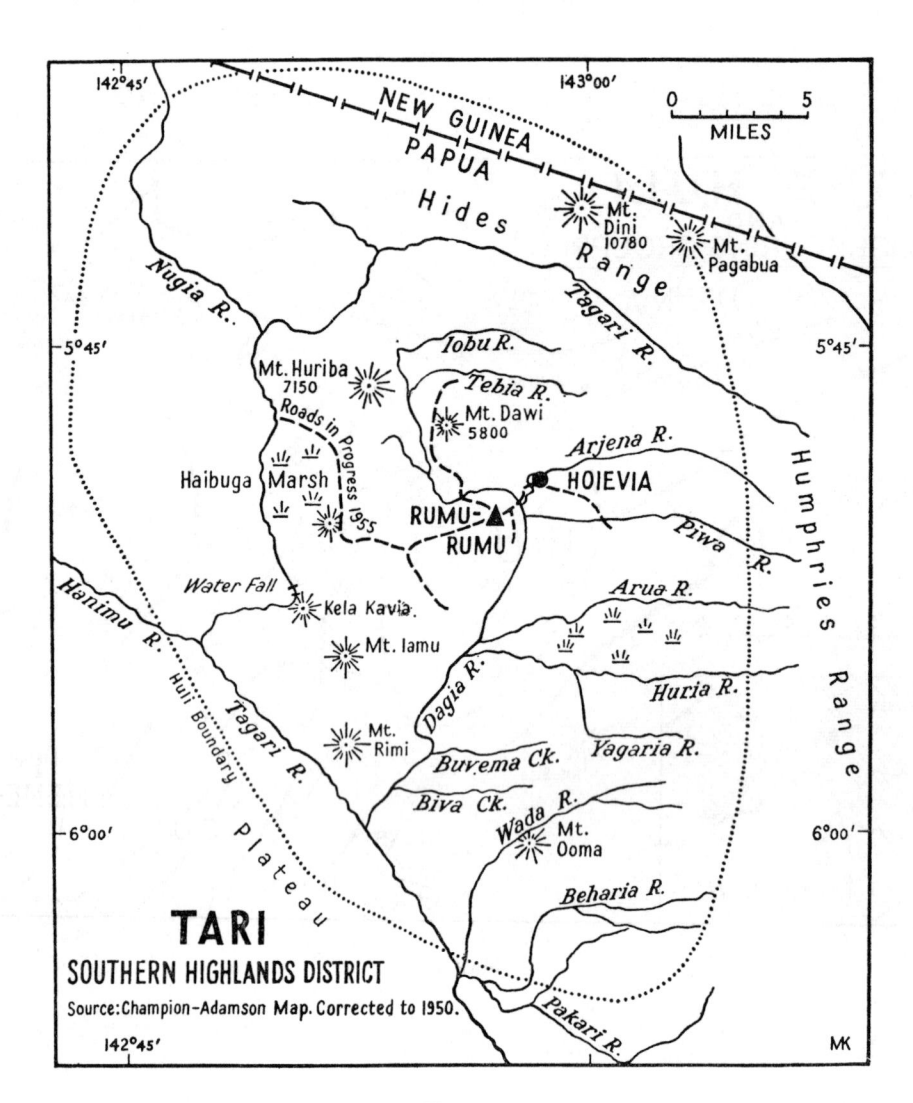

MAP 2.

Chapter I

INTRODUCTION

Discovery

In January, 1934 an Administration patrol set out to explore the mountainous country of central western Papua. Led by Jack Hides and Peter O'Malley, the party included ten Papuan constables and two dozen native carriers. Starting from the Upper Strickland River, they crossed the Great Papuan Plateau—an area sparsely inhabited by nomadic hunters—and climbed the limestone wastes of the Karius Range. In April, short of food and near exhaustion, the patrol discovered a populated highland valley. The people they had discovered were the Huli.

A description of the first meeting is given by Hides:

"Some of the inhabitants were in the fields below, and on calling to them, a number of short, stockily built men, all carrying bows and arrows, appeared not more than one hundred and fifty yards away. They looked at us queerly, with their heads to one side and appeared to be whispering excitedly among themselves; then they started to call . . . and soon we saw women and children hurrying across the fields (away from us)."[1]

Later the surprise and caution of the natives gave way to curiosity. A small group of men hesitantly approached the patrol's camp:

"They stood warily off us, not daring to allow us to touch them with a friendly hand . . . they had mops of brown hair adorned with

---

1. Hides 1936:79. (References are cited by the author's last name, the year of publication and the page. A full bibliography appears at the end of the volume.)

flowers. Three or four had rosettes of bachelor buttons; others had bands of eidelweiss across their foreheads; some had parrot feathers; while all of them had bone daggers stuck in the cane girdles around their waists. A knitted sporran, tucked between the cane girdles, was all the covering they had . . . their cheek bones were high, and their noses and lips finely moulded."[1]

No member of the patrol could understand the Huli language, but by use of signs the natives indicated that the Europeans could take food from their gardens. Hides offered them cloth and beads in return, but they were refused.

Next morning a man of imposing appearance approached the camp:

"He was a splendid figure of a man . . . with a black pointed beard, a cassowary quill through his nose and a carefully coiffured and flower decked (wig) . . . He appeared a very serious person, and when he came to a halt in front of O'Malley and myself . . . he looked at us very critically. He was silent for a minute, as he looked round at our tents and equipment; then he made . . . a speech. With his pantomime language . . . I could understand fairly clearly (what he was saying) . . . He appeared to be telling us that north, east and west were people in thousands—like the sands he picked up and let fall through his fingers. We were in a land of plenty. They did not want our steel—they had their own stone axes, which gave them all they wanted."[2]

Hides wanted to go eastwards, but there was no track, so at the insistence of the orator, he took a northerly path. Many armed natives watched the patrol depart. Hides was suspicious and warned the constables to move with caution. A creek cut across the track, and beyond it was a stone embankment—an ideal place for an ambush. Hides halted the patrol and waited. Soon an excited party of bowmen emerged from concealment and began to surround them. To avert an attack, Hides ordered the constables to fire a few shots into the air. The natives were frightened and fled.

Further up the valley, the patrol met several men who offered to act as guides, and for the next few days they passed through densely populated country. Although the people were friendly and gave the travellers food, Hides saw evidence of hostility and fighting among them. No guide would take the patrol beyond the confines of his own territory.

A few days later the patrol entered the central basin of the Tagari River. Here another group of Huli bowmen attacked them and

1. HIDES 1936:81.
2. HIDES 1936:83.

again they had to open fire. The patrol moved on, but the people were not hospitable, offering as food only a few stringy sweet potatoes.

Hide's patrol spent two weeks crossing Huli territory, a journey of about 120 miles. In some places they were welcomed by the curious inhabitants, in others they were vigorously attacked. The Huli were a volatile, excitable people, divided into numerous small groups that frequently engaged in warfare.

Early Contact

During the next twenty years, a few more patrols paid short visits to Huli territory, but their impact on native life was slight. It was not until 1951 that an Administration post was established at Rumurumu near the centre of the Tagari River Basin. Owing to a shortage of funds, this post was closed after two months. In April, 1952, it re-opened with a staff of one patrol officer and a medical assistant. Six months later, the Methodist Overseas Mission and the Unevangelized Fields Mission established stations at Tari.[1] At this time, only ten square miles of Huli territory were under administrative control and, except for patrol officers, no Europeans were permitted to live or travel more than two miles away from the patrol post. In 1955 a Roman Catholic missionary established a station, and in 1956 Seventh Day Adventist missionaries also began to build.

At the time of my first field trip (1955-56) the influence of the missions on Huli culture and society was not very great. The missionaries were pre-occupied with building their stations, attempting to learn the language and establishing schools. They did not attempt to discourage traditional rituals. There was no cannibalism to suppress, and apart from warfare, they felt that few Huli institutions were grossly repugnant to Christian ideals.

At the time of my second field trip (1959), the impact of the missions was still very limited. The Methodists—whom I knew best—had established a well-patronized medical aidpost and were building a leper hospital. Their religious services were fairly well attended, but indigenous rituals were still practised regularly.

The preservation of traditional institutions may also be attributed to the fact that Huli economy changed very little with the advent of the white man. No coffee planters entered the area, and there was a very limited market for introduced crops such as tomatoes, cabbages and peanuts.

1. Tari is the official name of the Administration Subdistrict centred at Rumurumu. It is not an indigenous name, but is probably an abbreviation of Tagari, the major river system which drains the area.

The persistence of Huli culture and social institutions can also be related to the isolation of the population. No roads connect Tari with the outside world, not even to the District headquarters at Mendi. Virtually all stores and supplies reach Tari by air, and the few Europeans who visit rarely venture beyond the station boundaries.

In 1958, the Tari Administration controlled about 100 square miles in the central Tagari basin and a second patrol post was established at Koroba. This new post was located about 50 miles northwest of Rumu-rumu, in a bilingual area where Huli and Duna are both spoken.[1]

Near these two centres of administration, warfare had been effectively suppressed. In other parts of Huli territory, fighting had been reduced but not eliminated by 1959. Some parts of Huli territory are still unexplored, and at present some Huli have not yet seen white men.

Distribution of the Population

According to the 1960 Administration Census, the population of Tari and Koroba Subdistricts numbered just over 41,000. All of the Tari population (21,955) and at least half of the Koroba population (19,112) can be regarded as Huli. Just where the dividing line—or zone of transition—between Huli and Duna culture is to be found, was still uncertain in 1959.

Table 1. The Size and Population of Tari and Koroba Census Divisions, 1960

Census division	Population Enumerated	Population Estimated	Total	Area Sq. miles	Density Persons Sq. miles
Tari Subdistrict:					
A. Haibuga-Munima	3,735	500	4,235	60	71
B. South Basin	259	1,500	1,759	110	16
C. North Basin	314	500	814	120	68
D. Central Basin	1,982	500	2,482	40	62
E. East Basin	1,280	500	1,780	210	8
F. Iumu	1,085	300	1,385	40	35
G. Pujero	—	3,000	3,000	70	43
H. Mananda	—	3,500	3,500	310	11
I. Lower Tagari	—	1,500	1,500	110	14
J. Benaria	—	1,500	1,500	150	10
Total	8,655	13,300	21,955	1,220	18

1. For an account of the opening, see Sinclair 1958a and 1958b.

INTRODUCTION

TABLE 1. *Continued*

Koroba Subdistrict:

K.	Koroba	3,112	4,000	7,112	160	44
L.	Mogorofugwa	—	3,500	3,500	60	58
M.	Lavani Valley	—	1,000	1,000	450	2
N.	Paru-Adzugari	—	5,000	5,000	80	62
O.	Upper Tumbuda	—	2,500	2,500	170	21
	Total	3,112	16,000	19,112	920	21
Grand total		11,767	29,300	41,067	2,140	19

The figures of Table 1 are largely estimated, yet it is clear that the overall density of population at Tari and Koroba is comparatively low—an average of only 19 persons per square mile. If uninhabited areas are omitted from the calculation, the effective density is doubled, but this figure is still moderate by highland standards. In the Central and North Basin Census Divisions, where I carried out fieldwork, densities of 68 and 62 persons per square mile are recorded. These figures are probably higher than they were before the establishment of the Tari patrol post, for the central basin was open to attack, and few people resided there permanently.

Accurate estimates of population are particularly difficult to make at Tari because the people do not live in villages. They live in small, strongly-built wooden houses scattered widely among their gardens. Huli men fear pollution as a result of contact with menstruating women, and they live in houses apart from their wives and children. The women's houses may be from 20 yards to 2 miles away from the men's.

COUNTRY AND CLIMATE

The Huli live in a series of broad valleys which together form the basin of the Tagari River. The general level of the basin floor is about 5,300 feet above sea level, and within this area few ridges exceed 8,000 feet. The country is open and gently undulating. The landscape is varied: stands of primary forest punctuate the neatly mounded gardens, reed covered swamps and kunai (Imperata) grasslands.

The climate is temperate. Temperatures rarely reach 27 °C or fall below 7 °C, and there is no seasonal variation. Annual rainfall averages 96 inches (1955-59), with a variation of about 20 per cent.

Rain falls on an average of 270 days a year, but there is no monthly pattern. Frost occurs about once or twice a decade, and it may lead to serious crop failure. Extreme fluctuations in rainfall—either too little or too much—occasionally lead to crop damage and temporary shortages of food. When this happens, the people migrate to the Waga or Ipili valleys until good times return.

The fauna of the area includes possums, tree kangaroos, wild pigs, snakes, eels, small fish, bats and many kinds of rodent. The species of birds include at least 16 varieties of bird of paradise. Pigs and dogs are the only domesticated animals.

The People

The Huli regard themselves as one people by virtue of their descent from a putative male ancestor called *Huli*. A son of spirit beings, he is said to have been the first man who gardened on Huli territory. People do not trace their genealogy step by step from this ancestor, but they speak of him as the 'father of all'. They say that the brothers of this ancestor founded the adjacent cultural groups: the Waga,[1] the Ipili,[2] the Duna,[3] and the Dugube,[4] and they exchange visits and occasionally intermarry with these people. Huli apply the term *Hewa* to little known peoples in remote areas. Before European contact, the Huli had no knowledge of the Mendi or Mae Enga, and no one—at least in the central basin—had journeyed to the Papuan lowlands.

The Huli language is spoken throughout Tari and in the eastern and southern portions of Koroba.[5] There are dialectical variations throughout the region, but all are mutually intelligible.

Unlike many highland peoples, the Huli are conscious of their cultural homogeneity and they are aware of the differences between their own social institutions and those of their neighbours. This cultural self-consciousness may be partly attributed to the mobility of the population. With no high mountain ranges to cross, travel is comparatively easy, and people often maintain two or three homesteads in different places.

---

1. WILLIAMS (1938) and MEGGITT (1956) have published accounts of the Waga, based on short field trips.
2. MEGGITT (1957a; 1958a) gave accounts of the Ipili, after a brief visit.
3. SINCLAIR, an Administration patrol officer, wrote an account of the opening of Duna territory (1958a, b).
4. No anthropologist has yet visited the Dugube, who are reported to be cannibals.
of Wurm classifies Huli as a sub-family of the Enga-Huli-Pole-Wiru Family
5. the East New Guinea Highland Stock (1961).

INTRODUCTION

Economic values are standardized throughout Huli territory. Pigs are the principal exchange commodity and form the basis of bride price, death indemnities and ritual payments. Cowrie and gold-lip shell, traded in from the north and east, function as currency for purchasing stone axe blades, native salt and string bags.

The subsistence economy is based on sweet potato cultivation. Using a swidden technique, Huli obtain high yields[1] from the volcanic soils. The most fertile soils produce a crop in three or four months, and it is not unusual to obtain two crops in one year. Huli also grow taro, bananas, sugar cane, beans, pumpkin and a variety of leaf vegetables. As there are no regular seasons, they garden all the year round, and there is little need for large-scale work groups.

Although Huli produce most of their goods locally, they trade with neighbouring peoples for a few of their requirements. They barter pigs with the Dugube for black-palm bows, and for stone axe blades from the Waga—blades that originate in quarries 20 miles West of Mt. Hagen. With cowrie shell they purchase salt from the Ipili and body oil from the Lake Kutubu area. Trade is not extensively organized; there is no regular market, and goods are bartered from group to group without the services of merchants.

As in most highland societies, Huli have no chiefs or hereditary offices vested with political authority. Leaders achieve status by their ability in war, skill in mediating disputes and by amassing wealth in pigs and shell. Disputes are settled by informal moots, oath-taking or by warfare.

The Problem

This thesis is a study of the application and significance of descent principles in Huli society. Huli reckon descent in most social activities. To validate a claim for land, a man cites his ancestors who gardened or were buried there. A brother allots shares of his sister's bride price on the basis of genealogical relationships. When war threatens, a man decides which side to support on the basis of descent ties, and he contributes to death indemnities on the same grounds. To bring an end to sickness caused by the ghost of a female ancestor, a man divines the ghost responsible and offers propitiatory gifts.

At first there appears to be a contradiction in the principles of descent recognized by the Huli. On the one hand, Huli insist that their politico-land owning groups are cognatically structured, that

---

1. Up to twelve tons per acre per year have been recorded for gardens after five years of continuous production.

all the descendants of a group founder, traced through males or females, are eligible for membership in the group. On the other hand, within these groups, Huli can distinguish agnates from other kinds of cognate, and evidence suggests that the rights of agnates are superior to those of non-agnates, at least in relation to land. My census figures show that most descent groups consist of agnates and non-agnatic cognates in the proportion of one to two. So it is pertinent to ask:

1. Is the descent system essentially an agnatic one in which non-agnates enjoy limited rights? If this is the case, how is the preponderance of non-agnates in the descent group to be explained?

2. Is the descent system a genuinely cognatic one in which men are free to participate in the affairs of their many descent groups? If this hypothesis is correct, then what factors explain the relatively high proportion of male agnates in most groups? Are there incentives for men to use their agnatic descent ties for group membership, or do they suffer some disadvantage by failing to do so?

The people provide no clear answers to these questions. Statements about how their descent principles apply—while relevant—are not a reliable guide to what actually happens. It is necessary to study the status of agnates and non-agnates empirically, and to determine whether observed differences in social behaviour are statistically significant.

Gradually it becomes clear that the contradiction is not a real one, that the system has a logic of its own, and that the recognition of agnatic status is a means of personal identification consistent with the functioning of a wide-range cognatic descent system.

Chapter II

FUNDAMENTALS OF GROUP STRUCTURE

Huli call their basic groupings *hamigini*, a term that means 'children of brothers', or more generally, 'descendants of brothers'. They employ this term in reference to two related kinds of grouping:

1. A purely genealogical unit consisting of all descendants through males and females from a putative ancestor.

2. A *de facto* social group named after, and recruited from the living members of such a genealogical unit.

In conversation, Huli can tell from context whether *hamigini* is used in the first or second sense. To avoid ambiguity, I distinguish between them. For the first connotation I use 'cognatic stock', as employed by Radcliffe-Brown;[1] for the second I apply Hogbin and Wedgwood's term 'parish', which they define as "the largest local group forming a political unit" whether it be unilinear, cognatic or based on other principles.[2] The advantage of the latter term is in its generality: a parish may be constituted in many ways, provided that it is a 'local' and a 'political' group.

'Local' and 'political' require some explanation. I call the parish local in a territorial rather than a residential sense. Every parish group owns a territory in common, though only a portion of its members lives or gardens there. The crucial point is that all parish members have rights in the territory of the group, whether or not they make use of them. It is in this special sense that the Huli parish is a local group.

The parish may be described as 'political' for a number of reasons. Firstly, it is a named group whose members see themselves as a unit

1. In RADCLIFFE-BROWN and FORDE 1950:15.
2. HOGBIN and WEDGWOOD 1953:243.

vis-à-vis like units. Secondly, its members ought to settle disputes peaceably, although they do not always do so. Thirdly, when any member is attacked, all feel some responsibility to repulse the invader. In this sense, the Huli parish is a political group.

Thus, the Huli parish may be defined tentatively as a cognatic group that owns territory in common, ideally settles internal disputes peaceably and mobilizes when threatened by enemies. This definition will be elaborated as the study progresses.

Huli also describe the sub-units of a parish as *hamigini*. They too are cognatic units; they own a sector of the parish-territory; they may be named after male or female ancestors; and their members are united by stronger jural ties than parish members of different sub-units. They are, in fact, the effective political units in Huli society. They wage war, make peace and pay indemnities independently. I call them *parish-sections*.

On rare occasions from two to eight parish groups co-ordinate rituals on the basis of common descent. Although the associations are named, Huli have no generic term for them. People say that they are parishes that have expanded, segmented and lost their political functions. The purpose of the association is to co-ordinate the sequence of rites rather than mobilize joint performance. I refer to these groupings as *parish-associations*.

A. Residence

Huli distinguish terminologically between resident and non-resident parish members. The former are called *bamba hene*, 'long time member' and the latter, *dagidia hene*, 'outside member'. Both residents and non-residents may or may not garden on parish-territory: the use of parish land is not crucial for membership. A non-resident member must satisfy the same conditions as a resident to retain his status. He must support the group in warfare, contribute to its indemnities and participate in its ritual. A non-resident member of one parish is generally a resident member of some other group (or groups) at the same time. It is a fundamental characteristic of the Huli system that an individual may belong simultaneously to several parish groups.

A resident member may reside unilocally or multilocally. A *unilocal* resident lives exclusively in one house, eating and sleeping there, and gardening nearby. Huli refer to him as *habo hene*, 'stable member'. He maintains only one homestead, though he may belong at the same time to other parish groups as a non-resident member.

A *multilocal* resident lives for a few days or weeks on one parish-territory, then moves to another in a more or less regular sequence. He maintains two, or occasionally three homesteads. He lives at each for periods determined by the size and location of his gardens, the pressure of parish affairs and his personal wishes. Huli graphically describe such residents as *inya pu ibu*, 'those who come and go'.

If the parish-territories of a bilocal resident are close, he may commute between them on a daily basis. He may keep his pigs in one, where it is marshy, and cultivate land on the river flats of another. The wives of a polygynist often live on different parish-territories. Women too may be multilocal residents, but those with several small children are more likely to live unilocally. In the comparatively open country where they live, Huli prefer multilocal residence, for it ensures them asylum in several groups.

A man can freely change his mode and place of residence. A unilocal resident can move to another parish-territory where he has dormant rights, or he may become a bilocal resident. A man may become a member of any parish group with which he is genealogically affiliated, provided the group is willing to accept him. The parish generally welcomes a newcomer, but he must prove his loyalty before he acquires full rights in the group.

In relation to the parish-territory, members may be classified as non-residents, unilocal residents or multilocal residents. None of these categories implies that a man belongs to only one parish at a time. A unilocal resident may belong to other parish groups as a non-resident. A non-resident is always a resident of some parish. A multilocal resident may, in addition, be a non-resident member of other parish groups.

B. Descent Affiliation of Parish Members

A second classification of parish members is by mode of affiliation. Members may be classed as (1) cognatic descendants of the parish-founder, called *damene*, literally 'kin', and (2) 'others', *tare*, which includes affines and unrelated friends of parish-members.

Agnates are distinguished terminologically from other kinds of cognate. They are called *tene damene*, in contrast to *yamuwini damene*, kin related through female ties. These terms also apply to men qualified by descent, who are not actual members. Thus, everyone has agnatic status with respect to some particular parish, whether or not he uses it to acquire membership. In the same way, a man is also a non-agnatic cognate of several other parish-groups. No two individuals, except siblings, are affiliated with the same set of parish-groups.

Huli classify cognates other than agnates according to their relationship to the patrilineal ancestors of the parish. The sons and daughters of a female agnate are called *ainyia damene*, 'mother-related kin'. Their children in turn, are called *agua damene*, 'grandmother-related kin', which applies to both paternal and maternal grandchildren. The same principle is employed in successive generations. Children of *agua damene* are called *aguanani damene*, and trace their relationship to patrilineal ancestors through a great-grandmother. In this case, there are four possible descent links: the FaMoMo, the FaFaMo, the MoFaMo or the MoMoMo. In the next generation, great-great-grandchildren are called *aburi*, and their descent tie comes through one of eight ancestresses: the FaFaFaMo, FaFaMoMo, FaMoMoMo, FaMoFaMo, MoMoMoMo, MoFaFaMo, MoMoFaMo and the MoFaMoMo. Finally, Huli apply the term *aguaneli* where the female tie to a patrilineal ancestor is more than four generations removed from Ego. Thus, non-agnates are distinguished according to a simple principle—the generation of the ancestress who links a person to the patrilineal ancestors of the group.[1]

These principles of classification are not always relevant to social behaviour. When warfare threatens, the parish mobilizes without regard to the descent status of individual members—agnates do not fight as a separate unit. Yet, there are social situations where descent determines behaviour. In the complex fertility rite called the *Tege*, the sponsoring unit is led by two men, one of whom must be an agnate, and who receives payment from the non-agnates of the group. The other must be affiliated to the group through a female tie, and for his services the agnates pay an equal amount.

One further distinction is sometimes made among the cognatic members of the parish. Certain non-agnates are described as 'like agnates', *tene hamene*. They must be descended through three or more patrilineal links from a female agnatic ancestor of the group. I call them *quasi-agnates*. Genealogically, they are like agnates, save that their descent line from the group apical ancestor contains one female link. In certain contexts they are socially identified with agnates.

Non-cognates, who include affines and unrelated friends, may also acquire limited rights from the parish. I refer to an affine related by a current or recent marriage as a *direct affine*, and an affine related to the group by a tie several generations back as an *indirect affine*. Huli call unrelated friends *igity yango*.

1. This system of classification is similar in principle to that described by HOGBIN for Malaita (1939:28). Malaita districts are also cognatic, but "there is a word for persons to whom an individual is related through males, *ainifasia*. The children of womenfolk of this group are called *ngwaikwalina*, and their children, again *mburi*."

C. Parish Composition

In the central Tari basin, I recorded the names of 61 parish groups. There may well be 100 more groups outside the basin. I took an intensive census of five parish groups, and record some of the results in Table 2. For the sake of clarity, this table includes only adult males over the apparent age of 20. Wives and children will be tabulated later.

Before analysing the figures, it is necessary to explain how the census was taken. It is difficult to take a census where each person may belong to several groups and moves freely from one territory to another. I conducted house-to-house surveys on each parish-territory, but inevitably some multilocal residents and many non-resident members of the sample groups were absent and could not be interviewed. It was necessary, therefore, to take lists of absentees from members who were available. In part this proved satisfactory, but informants sometimes disagreed as to whether certain men should be included as members. Some men recalled occasions when the disputed members had failed in their parish duties. Others countered with instances when they had acted appropriately. To decide whether or not to include doubtful members, I had to take the consensus of available members as a guide.[1]

Table 2. The Adult Male Members of Five Parish Groups, 1959

			Parish				
Category	A	B	C	D	E	Total	Per cent
Residents :							
— Unilocal:							
Agnates	9	4	4	6	12	35	5.3
Non-agnatic cognates:*							
Mo	1	3	2	1	3	10	
FaMo	1	3	1	—	4	9	
MoMo	1	1	3	2	2	9	
Other	8	3	3	7	10	31	
Sub-total	*11*	*10*	*9*	*10*	*19*	*59*	*9.0*

* *(See p. 29.)*

1. I discuss the implication of this in Chapter v.

TABLE 2. *Continued*

Non-cognates:							
Direct affines	3	3	2	1	—	9	
Indirect affines	1	4	1	1	5	12	
Friends	—	1	—	—	1	2	
Sub-total	*4*	*8*	*3*	*2*	*6*	*23*	*3.5*
All unilocal	*24*	*22*	*16*	*18*	*37*	*117*	*17.8*
Multilocal:							
Agnates	16	5	5	10	25	61	9.3
Non-agnatic cognates:							
Mo	1	8	9	5	8	31	
FaMo	9	—	3	4	8	24	
MoMo	4	—	3	2	3	12	
Other	36	3	8	15	32	94	
Sub-total	*50*	*11*	*23*	*26*	*51*	*161*	*24.6*
Non-cognates:							
Direct affines	4	2	8	2	6	22	
Indirect affines	1	6	6	11	3	27	
Friends	2	1	1	2	1	7	
Sub-total	*7*	*9*	*15*	*15*	*10*	*56*	*8.5*
All multilocal	*73*	*25*	*43*	*51*	*86*	*278*	*42.4*
Total residents	*97*	*47*	*59*	*69*	*123*	*395*	*60.2*
Non-residents:							
Agnates	6	8	11	5	5	35	5.3
Non-agnatic cognates:							
Mo	9	4	5	4	10	32	
FaMo	8	12	6	2	6	34	
MoMo	8	—	14	4	7	33	
Other	16	1	10	17	15	59	
Sub-total	*41*	*17*	*35*	*27*	*38*	*158*	*24.1*
Non-cognates:							
Direct affines	11	5	7	11	15	49	
Indirect affines	4	3	2	—	4	13	
Friends	3	—	2	—	1	6	
Sub-total	*18*	*8*	*11*	*11*	*20*	*68*	*10.4*

TABLE 2. *Continued*

Total non-residents		65	33	57	43	63 261	39.8
Grand total		162	80	116	112	186 656	100.0

* The table does not include all the Huli sub-categories of non-agnatic cognate. Whereas informants could indicate their own genealogical connections to the parish, they were uncertain of the exact relationships of absent members, particularly those related to the parish agnatic core through distant female ties. Consequently, I classified non-agnatic cognates as related to a parish patrilineal ancestor through the mother, father's mother, mother's mother and through any 'other' female ties.

Analysis of Table 2 yields a number of generalizations about the structure and composition of the parish.[1] The number of men per parish ranges from 80 to 186, and the average size is 133 men. If we include women and children resident on parish-territory, the average parish size is about 500 persons, and ranges roughly from 270 to 700.

Of male parish members, 60.2 per cent are resident members, while 39.8 are non-residents. In every parish, residents outnumber non-residents in roughly the same proportions. The parish, therefore, is only partly a residential group.

Of parish residents, 30 per cent reside unilocally, and 70 per cent multilocally. Taking residents and non-residents together, 17.8 per cent are unilocal, and 42.4 per cent multilocal residents. This shows that only a small proportion of parish members reside exclusively on parish territory. The figures emphasize an important characteristic of the descent system—men belong simultaneously to several groups.

The figures also show that each parish has some members who are agnates, some non-agnatic cognates and some non-cognates, the overall proportions being 19.9 per cent, 57.7 per cent and 22.4 per

---

1. Throughout this study, I employ the chi square test to determine if observed distributions differ significantly from hypothetical ones. For example, the above distribution of agnates, non-agnatic cognates and non-cognates can be compared with a hypothetical distribution in which an equal number of men are found in each category. The result of the computation is that chi square = 172. Since the data contain 2 degrees of freedom, the probability that the observed distribution is a chance variation from the hypothetical one is less than 1 in 100. Thus, we conclude that the observations represent a genuine pattern, and that taking additional observations is not likely to alter it significantly. Whenever I employ the chi square test, I report the computed value of chi square, the number of degrees of freedom (df), and the probability value (p) as determined from the Tables.

cent respectively. In every parish there are some agnates who are unilocal residents, some who are multilocal residents and some non-residents, and non-agnatic cognates are distributed in the same way.

It is difficult to discover from Table 2 whether there is a significant association between descent and residence. Are agnates more often unilocal residents than multilocal? Or is a non-agnatic member more likely to be a non-resident than a resident member? These questions can be answered by re-arranging the data in Table 2 and applying statistical tests.

TABLE 3. ANALYSIS OF ASSOCIATION BETWEEN RESIDENCE AND MODE OF AFFILIATION

Categories	Agnates	Non-agnatic cognates	Non-cognates	Total	Significance
1.					
Unilocal residents	35	59	23	117	chi squared = 4.9,
Multilocal residents	61	161	56	278	df = 2, p > .05
Total	*96*	*220*	*79*	*395*	
2.					
Residents	96	220	79	395	chi squared = 10.16,
Non-residents	35	158	68	261	df = 2, p < .01
Total	*131*	*378*	*147*	*656*	
3.		*(All Non-Agnates)*			
Residents	96	299		395	chi squared = 9.9
Non-residents	35	226		261	df = 2, p < .01, ø = .12
Total	*131*	*525*		*656*	

The following conclusions may be drawn:

1. There is no significant association between being an agnate and being a unilocal resident. In other words, the residentially stable members of the parish are just as likely to be non-agnates as agnates.

2. There is some association between a person's descent affiliation and his residence or non-residence.[1]

---

1. Part 3 of the Table combines columns 2 and 3 to measure the extent of the association. In this form the phi coefficient (ø), which is a measure of the degree of correlation between two variables, can be computed.

FUNDAMENTALS OF GROUP STRUCTURE

3. There is a significant association between being an agnate and being a resident, but the strength of the association is low. In other words, agnates tend to be resident members only slightly more often than they are non-resident members.

The major point is that a person's mode of affiliation to a parish bears little relation to his residential behaviour. The parish is not a group with a nucleus of agnates who are residentially stable, while non-agnates come and go. Rather, the evidence suggests that descent ties are not particularly important in determining whether a man resides unilocally, multilocally, or outside the group-territory.

D. Tunda Parish—A Detailed Example

Deeper insight into parish structure can be gained by examining one group (*A* in Table 2) in greater detail. Tunda parish is one that I have studied closely, and part of its genealogy appears in Figure 1.

Genealogy of Tunda to the Parish-Section Level.

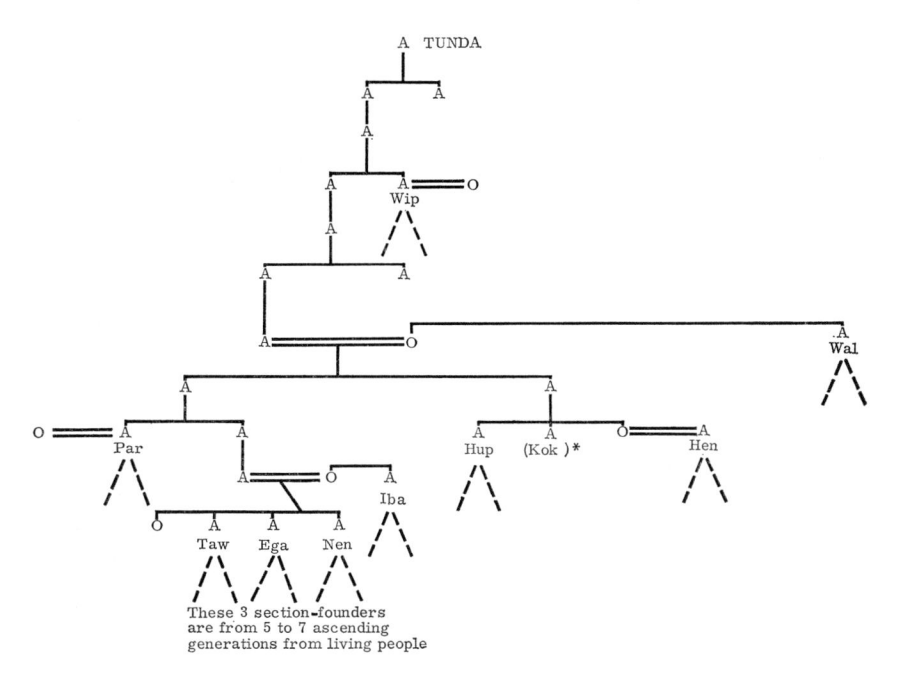

* Kok is an obsolete section; only one living descendant, a non-agnatic cognate is known, and he is a boy living with Nen kinsmen. For convenience, section names are abbreviated.

At first sight, the genealogy appears to be that of a unilineal descent group. This is not the case. Five of the section-founders, Wip, Par, Hup, Taw and Ega, are agnatic descendants from Tunda, but Iba, Hen and Wal are not. Hen section is named after the husband of a female agnate—thus in this section no one can be an agnate descended from Tunda. Wal and Iba sections are headed by brothers-in-law of female agnates, and their members are not cognatic descendants of Tunda at all, although members of other sections regard them as such. In fact, few members of any Tunda section can fully trace the above genealogy. Most men distinguish simply between sections founded by agnates *(hamigini tene)* and sections related to the patrilineal ancestors through female ties *(hamigini yamuwini)*.

Earlier, I defined an indirect affine as a person related to the patrilineal parish ancestors through a marriage more than three generations in the past. Technically, all members of Iba and Hen belong in this category, but they have gradually achieved the jural status of distinct sections. Six other indirect affines are members of the parish. They are scattered among the Wip, Par, Ega and Taw sections. All of them are descended from sisters of Wip, Par, Ega and Taw, nevertheless their membership in the group is uncontested.

TABLE 4. MEN OF TUNDA PARISH, BY SECTION, 1959

Category	Nen	Taw	Hup	Ega	Iba	Wip	Par	Hen	Wal	Total
Resident:										
Agnates	18	0	4	0	0	1	2	0	0	25
Non-agnatic cognates	13	8	6	5	5	1	12	10	1	61
Non-cognates	7	0	1	0	0	1	2	0	0	11
Sub-total	38	8	11	5	5	3	16	10	1	97
Non-resident:										
Agnates	2	2	2	0	0	0	0	0	0	6
Non-agnatic cognates	5	7	5	6	4	3	6	5	0	41
Non-cognates	6	2	3	1	1	1	3	1	0	18
Sub-total	13	11	10	7	5	4	9	6	0	65
Total	51	19	21	12	10	7	25	16	1	162

Wal section consists of one senile man only, who lives with Hen men, and has been accepted as a member of Hen. Thus, Tunda parish contains eight sections, ranging in size from 7 to 51 men, an average of 20 men per section.

So far, the discussion has been limited to men. When we try to include women and children, problems of classification arise. The wives and children of a man do not always live on his parish-territory, and they do not necessarily follow him from place to place. For example, the wife of a multilocal resident may be a unilocal resident, and she may not live on any of his parish-territories. In such instances it is confusing to count a man's dependants as members of his parish. In Table 5, I record the male and female residents (unilocal and multilocal) of Tunda parish, and the non-resident wives and children of resident members.

TABLE 5. THE RESIDENTS OF TUNDA PARISH-TERRITORY, BY SECTION, 1959

Category	Nen	Taw	Hup	Ega	Iba	Wip	Par	Hen	Wal	Total
Males :										
Married	33	5	9	4	4	2	14	6	1	78
Single (over 15)	5	3	3	1	1	1	2	3	—	19
Boys (under 15)	29	1	5	1	5	3	10	7	—	61
All Males	*67*	*9*	*17*	*6*	*10*	*6*	*26*	*16*	*1*	*158*
Females :										
Married (Hu. resident)	17	6	5	2	3	6	14	6	—	59
Married (Hu. non-resident)	3	1	—	1	—	2	4	1	—	12
Single (over 15)	2	1	—	—	—	1	2	1	—	7
Widows	1	1	—	—	1	1	1	—	—	5
Divorcees	—	—	—	—	1	—	1	—	—	2
Girls (under 15)	27	7	4	1	2	2	9	7	2	61
All females	*50*	*16*	*9*	*4*	*7*	*12*	*31*	*15*	*2*	*146*
Total	*117*	*25*	*26*	*10*	*17*	*18*	*57*	*31*	*3*	*304*
Non-resident wives and children under 15 years of above men :										
Wives	18	4	3	—	1	—	7	4	1	38
Boys	4	5	5	1	—	2	4	9	—	30
Girls	20	4	4	—	1	1	6	1	—	37
All	*42*	*13*	*12*	*1*	*2*	*3*	*17*	*14*	*1*	*105*

These figures reveal that the elementary family is not a sub-unit of the parish in a residential sense. The 79 married men have a total of 59 co-resident wives and 38 non-resident wives. Of their 196 children (under the age of about 15), 66 per cent are co-resident and 34 per cent are non-resident. Twelve married women reside on Tunda territory whose husbands do not. Ten of these wives reside multilocally, alternating between their husbands' territories and their own. Two reside unilocally, while their husbands live on nearby parish-territories.[1]

Examination of the figures in Tables 4 and 5 shows that the genealogical depth of a parish-section has little relationship, if any, to its size. The largest section Nen is comparatively shallow in depth, whereas Wip, the oldest section, has few members. This is not surprising in view of the continual changes in membership. After a defeat in war, an entire section may disperse, abandoning its territory. Some members may return in time, while others never do so.

E. Summary and Discussion

This chapter describes some basic characteristics of the Huli parish. The parish is defined as a cognatic group that owns a territory in common, and acts in a political capacity. The parish is composed of sections defined in genealogical terms, which also own territory. The section is the effective political unit; it wages war, makes peace and pays indemnities. Sections of one parish should settle disputes peaceably, but failing this, should not fight with lethal weapons. Parish groups tracing common descent associate to co-ordinate certain rites that occur once or twice a generation.

Not all parish members live on parish-territory. A non-resident acquires membership by fulfilling the same obligations as a resident member—defence of the group in war, contribution to its indemnities and participation in its rites. A unilocal resident maintains one domicile, whereas a multilocal resident shifts back and forth between two or more parish groups as a member of each. A man may be a member of several parish groups at the same time.

Every cognatic descendant from the founder of a parish is eligible for parish membership. Agnates are terminologically distinguished from non-agnatic cognates, but descent status is relevant to social behaviour only in certain contexts. Affines and unrelated persons can also acquire membership.

There is no significant association between being an agnate and unilocal residence, and only a very slight association between being an agnate and being a resident (as against non-resident). It seems

1. A full discussion of family residential patterns is given in Chapter IV.

that the parish has no stable agnatic core, though further evidence is necessary to prove this.

Models are sometimes helpful in interpreting complex social data. The observed data can be compared with a purely cognatic model in which the hypothetical ratio of agnates to non-agnatic cognates would be 1 to 1,024, assuming the apical ancestor of the group is 10 generations removed. The observed distribution, however, is 1 to 5, a statistically significant variation. Although the parish has agnatic bias, it is still fundamentally a cognatic unit. Agnatic bias does not make the Huli system an agnatic one.

What factors can be adduced to explain this bias? Do agnates enjoy benefits or privileges denied to other cognates? Informants' statements alone cannot answer this question. While the views of the people are important, they must be interpreted in the light of actual social behaviour.

Chapter III

LAND TENURE

A. Land Resources

Arable land at Tari is both plentiful and productive. Large tracts of land suitable for cultivation are still under forest, and many marshy areas could be drained by techniques known to inhabitants. Population density is low—only 18 persons per square mile in the whole sub-district, and only 68 per square mile in the most densely settled Census Division.[1] By comparison, central Enga average 120 persons per square mile,[2] and some Chimbu groups average 380 per square mile.[3] Sweet potato yields are about 10 tons per acre per year—a figure more than twice that of Central Enga.[4] The exceptional productivity of Huli gardens can be attributed to a number of factors. The soils are volcanic.[5] No high ranges deflect the sun, and gardens receive ample sunlight. Rain falls throughout the year, and frost seldom occurs. Finally, Huli gardeners make use of composting and drainage, and they mix ash with the soil before planting.

Huli rarely wage war in order to acquire land, and after a battle the victor seldom occupies the loser's territory. Groups occasionally fight about the boundaries of their territories, but few individuals quarrel seriously about garden claims. The low incidence of land disputes reflects the adequacy of Huli resources.

1. See Table 1, p. 13.
2. MEGGITT, 1958:256.
3. BROWN and BROOKFIELD, 1959:25.
4. MEGGITT, 1958.
5. Myths tell of white silt, called *Bingi*, falling from the sky about 100 years ago. It covered gardens and clogged the streams, but afterwards the gardens were much more productive.

B. Principles of Land-Holding

The Huli attitude toward land can be characterised in the following way. Men do not state "This land belongs to me—I own it". They say rather, "I belong to this land—my rights are here". A man often changes his place of residence and his garden sites, but parish boundaries are permanent.[1]

A land tenure system based on cognatic descent is possible where arable land is productive and in good supply. Huli can afford to be flexible in allocating land rights. Their rules of tenure are not codified elaborately, nor are they rigidly adhered to. No one is short of land. If a dispute occurs, it is generally settled without bloodshed by negotiation and compromise.

The basic principle of Huli land tenure is that land passes from its first owner (a parish founder) to all his descendants, male and female. The potential number of living descendants is very large, for according to genealogy and legend, the first ancestors lived from 12 to 18 generations ago. The principle, however, is subject to limitations, and in fact few parish groups have more than 100 land-holding members.

Huli distinguish between the specific rights of a person in a particular plot and the general rights of all cognates in the parish-territory at large. I refer to the former as a *title*—the legitimate right of a person to use, enjoy and dispose of property in land. I speak of the latter as an *interest* in the parish estate—a qualification based on descent to hold parish land. A person with an interest in the parish can acquire a title; it takes time and effort, for he must fulfil the obligations of parish membership.

A land title may be held individually or in common. Where land is held in common, the consent of the majority of title-holders is needed to use or dispose of the property. When a man dies, his common rights pass to his heirs.

Huli recognise that the rights of title may be divided unequally between two parties. One party, whom I call the *provisional title-*

---

1. Parish boundaries often follow watercourses or ridge lines. In some places, boundaries are marked by v-shaped ditches, 15 to 20 feet deep and 6 to 8 feet across at the top. Along the edges, men plant thickets of cane grass as a screen against arrows. The ditches also serve as passageways between parish-territories; they can be sealed off at strategic points in time of danger. In a few places boundaries are not permanent. Huli describe these areas as 'sharp teeth country' *(ne tebene dindi)*, because defending them is difficult. Before the arrival of the Administration, people did not settle permanently in these areas. If a man harvested a crop or two before fighting broke out, he counted himself fortunate.

holder, obtains use and possession of the land. The other, the *residual title-holder*, retains the rights of disposal, which include the power to repossess the property. If a provisional title-holder voluntarily relinquishes his rights, they revert automatically to the residual title-holder.

By custom, the land rights of women are limited. A woman does not usually hold full title. The few strong-minded widows or divorcees who choose not to remarry are exceptions. A woman can hold provisional title to land, provided that a man (or men) controls the residual rights. For example, a sister sometimes holds provisional title to land controlled by her brother. In Huli society then, men control the disposal of land regardless of the form of title (individual, joint or common) in which it is held, and regardless of how the title may be divided.

C. Validating Claims and Transferring Titles

Huli have no written registers or deeds, but they have institutionalized means of validating claims and transferring titles. When a boy is about eight, his parents show him the location of gardens in which he has potential rights. His father points out the boundaries of his gardens, the grave sites of ancestors buried there and the trees he and his ancestors have planted. He also tells his son of the other parish groups in which he holds potential rights, rights which he or his ancestors have used in the past. In the same way, a woman shows her son the boundaries of her current gardens and the location of other plots where she gardened before. If necessary, she consults her kinsmen to find what rights have passed down from her ancestors.

A man's strongest claims are to the gardens, on any parish-territory, that his father cultivates and holds in full title. His matrilateral claims are not quite as strong, for he needs the consent of maternal kinsmen in order to acquire full title.

In adolescence, a youth begins to cultivate his own gardens. His father encourages him in this by giving him a plot of his own. The youth works the garden by himself, but he cannot dispose of the title without his father's permission. Similarly, a boy acquires land from his maternal grandfather. The longer he makes use of it, the more secure is his right. When his father or uncle dies, the youth inherits residual rights and thereby acquires full title.

As he approaches old age, a man distributes his titles among his sons and nephews. He may give each a specific garden, but more often he gives them joint rights, leaving them to arrange the details as they see fit. A divided title implies a close social relationship, so when a man dies, his residual rights pass to the provisional title-holder rather than to his heirs. When a provisional owner dies, his rights may pass to his heirs or they may be recovered by the residual title-holder. There is no fixed rule—the outcome depends on the relationships between the heirs and the residual title-holders. They seldom dispute how the rights should be distributed, just as co-heirs seldom quarrel about the division of their inheritance.

It often happens that a parish-section leaves its territory following defeat in war. Members of other sections of the same parish then occupy this land pending their return. The land is acquired on the basis of common parish rights. Again, usage and the passage of time tend to sanctify the possessor's right; the longer the original owners stay away, the more difficult it becomes for them to recover their property. In this way, a provisional title tends to become a full title. Although the residual title-holder does not formally relinquish his rights, they atrophy through disuse.

A man with a general interest in parish land (by virtue of descent) can convert it to a specific title. He must first authenticate his claim by tracing his descent, step by step, from a parish ancestor. If he can show where his ancestors were buried and where they cultivated gardens, it strengthens his claim. Generally, he can acquire title to unused parish land without difficulty. He requires only consent of the group that holds common rights in the land. Provided the group accepts him as a member, he gains full title by using the land. A man also acquires title by requesting provisional rights from a full owner. He applies to a close friend or kinsman; he does not pay for the rights, but receives them freely on the basis of a social relationship.[1]

D. Tunda Land-Holding

A detailed example will illustrate the principles of land tenure. Map 3 shows land-holding and land use in the territory of Tunda parish, which is located in the Central Basin Census Division. As the key shows, the map is divided into three sections. Using pace and compass traverses, I mapped the first sector completely, and searched the titles to all of its gardens. I did not map the second sector in detail, but I measured all gardens and investigated their titles. No current or recent gardens are found north of Porami Ridge, the third sector. This is an area of forested slopes and kunai grassland where

---

1. When a man needs food unexpectedly (when he receives a large payment of pigs), he can buy a crop of sweet potato without obtaining any rights to the garden plot.

LAND TENURE 41

some Tunda men keep pigs, but most avoid it, preferring the richer soils near the Adyena River and the safety of proximity to the government station.

The letters in the map which precede garden numbers indicate the parish-section of the full or residual title-holder. The code is as follows: A represents Nen section, B—Par, C—Ega, D—Hup, E—Hen, F—Taw and G—Wip.[1] Letters underlined indicate that the title is divided between a provisional and residual title-holder.

The map indicates a number of ways in which land may be held in common. One possibility is divided ownership in which individuals hold provisional titles while residual titles are held by a group in common. The tongue of land containing gardens B35 to B61 is an example. This piece of land has an interesting history. About three or four generations ago, a son of the section-founder, Par, gave the land to matrilateral kinsmen in the adjacent parish-territory of Mataba. The descendants of the son of Par contended that provisional rights only were given, and they sought to recover possession by litigation. Mataba men denied the claim and insisted that they held full title. The disputed area measures only two acres, but it is valuable as the soil is rich from repeated flooding, and good sweet potato slips can always be obtained from it. Several years passed without settlement of the issue. Finally, the Mataba men agreed to relinquish the land in exchange for 7 pigs and 3 ropes of cowrie shell. The descendants of the original owner, having regained full title, divided it in the following way: they granted provisional rights to members of their own group and to a few others nominated by members, but they retained the residual rights in common. Thus, as a group, they hold firm control over this newly acquired and highly valued land. It is uncertain what will happen in the future, but informants say that the residual rights will gradually diminish in importance, and provisional rights will become full titles.

A second possibility is that a group holds full title in common. This is often the case with uncultivated parish land.[2] Any member may use such land, and thereby acquire full title. Tunda land north of the Porami Ridge is an example of uncultivated parish common. It is many years since it was gardened, and now only common rights are recognised. If a full title-holder makes no use of his property, his rights revert to the group.

1. See the genealogy on p. 31.
2. The distinction between fallow and uncultivated land is not always apparent to an observer. Garden fallow can sometimes be detected by the presence of banana and casuarina trees. The people are aware of the distinction. Land in fallow is generally held individually, whereas the rights to uncultivated land are held in common.

Land used for ritual is also held in common. The forest land between gardens A69b and A61 is an example. It is owned in common by Nen, Taw and Ega sections. Each group owns stone artefacts which are buried there, and no one cultivates the land because of its ritual associations. The area labelled 'cult ground' near garden A44 is another example. It is a secluded area, taboo to women and married men, where young bachelors undergo ritual training.[1] The surrounding forest is also parish common.

Many individuals own several titles to parish land. Hariwa, an agnate of Nen section, holds full title to eight gardens (A4, 7, 9, 11, 15, 19, 20 and 73), a total of 2.7 acres. Half of this area is under cultivation. He has granted provisional rights in two gardens (A16 and 74) to a sister and her husband; in due course her sons will inherit these titles. Hariwa gave provisional rights in another garden (A17) to his FaMoDa and her husband, an affinal member of Tunda parish, and to his FaFaFaSsDaSn, a 13 year old orphan whose father belonged to Nen section. Finally, he gave provisional rights in two gardens (A22 and 43) to a classificatory cross-cousin, the son of a female agnate of another section (Ega) of Tunda parish. Hariwa himself holds no provisional titles to Tunda territory.

Poge, another Nen agnate, has more limited holdings. He owns full title to six gardens (A3, 12, 21, 43, 60 and 72), a total of 1.6 acre, and he holds joint residual rights with another Nen agnate in a .5 acre garden (A22), the provisional owner of which is Wadulu, the son of a female agnate of Ega section.

Lebogia, the son of a Nen female agnate, holds full rights in four gardens (not shown on the map), totalling 1.1 acre. He is the residual title-holder to a garden of .2 acre, which is provisionally held by his cross-cousin, Wagia, a Nen agnate. He also holds provisional rights in a garden held residually by Andogia, a non-agnatic cognate of Taw section.

These examples illustrate the fragmentation of individual holdings, and those who are eligible to hold provisional rights in land. In Appendix 1, I give the full range of relationships between provisional and residual title-holders to Tunda gardens.

Not all members of Tunda parish garden on its territory. Only 79 of the 162 members hold controlling interests, that is, full or residual titles to parish land. By comparing the number of members who

---

1. At any given time 4 or 5 bachelors in their early twenties belong to the cult. They may be members of any parish-section, and they remain in the cult for 2 to 3 years. They spend a few days every month in the cult area, performing purificatory rites and cultivating a type of bog-iris, said to have magical properties. A permanent bachelor leads the cult and imbues the young men with ideals of self-reliance and pre-marital chastity. The aim of the cult is to promote the health and growth of its members.

hold titles with the number who do not, the association between status and land-holding can be tested.

TABLE 6. COMPARISON OF TUNDA PARISH MEMBERS WITH AND WITHOUT TITLES TO LAND ON TUNDA PARISH-TERRITORY

	Categories	Men with land*	Men without land	Total	Significance
1.	Cognates	73	60	133	chi squared = 11.1,
	Non-cognates	6	23	29	df = 1, p < .01, ø = .26
	Total	79	83	162	
2.	Agnates	23	8	31	chi squared = 6.06,
	Non-agnatic cognates	50	52	102	df = 1, .02 > p > .01, ø = .21
	Total	73	60	133	
3.	Unilocal residents	17	7	24	chi squared = 9.0,
	Multilocal residents	38	35	73	df = 2, p = .1
	Non-residents	24	41	65	
	Total	79	83	162	

* Either in full or residual title or in both.

The tests all reveal significant associations.

1. The chances are about equal that cognatic parish members will or will not hold land, but a non-cognate has only one chance in four.

2. The probability that an agnate will own land is about three to one in his favour, whereas the chances for a non-agnatic cognate are about equal.

3. A unilocal resident is twice as likely to own land as not, whereas the chances are one to two against a multilocal resident owning land. The probability is poorer still for a non-resident; he has only one chance in three of holding a title. Thus, residence is an important factor in acquiring title to land.

As it is possible that the *amount* of land held in title varies significantly with descent or residence, it is necessary to survey the extent of land-holding and the status of parish members. In Appendix II, I give detailed figures of the acreage held by the 79 Tunda title-holders, and in Table 7 below, I give a summary.

TABLE 7A. DESCENT AND THE EXTENT OF TUNDA LAND-HOLDING

Category	No. of Men	Acreage	Mean Acres per Man
Agnates	23	44.7	1.94
Non-agnatic cognates	50	46.8	.94
Non-cognates	6	1.8	.30
Total	79	93.3	1.18

Chi squared = 8.82, df = 2, .02 < p < .05.

TABLE 7B. RESIDENCE AND THE EXTENT OF TUNDA LAND-HOLDING

Unilocal residents	17	28.7	1.69
Multilocal residents	38	47.9	1.26
Non-residents	24	16.7	.70
Total	79	93.3	1.18

Chi squared = 4.26, df = 2, p > .05.

The table shows[1] that cognates own significantly more land than non-cognates. More importantly, it demonstrates that agnates hold significantly greater acreages than non-agnatic cognates. Thus, agnatic bias operates in two respects; among *parish members* more agnates are land-holders than non-land-holders, and among *land-holders*, the amount of land held by agnates is greater than the amount held by non-agnates.

Earlier I mentioned that among *parish members*, mode of residence is a significant prerequisite for land-holding. However, among land-holders, residence is not a significant factor, for the observed variations are not statistically significant. In other words, a man's style of residence affects his chances of holding parish land, but it does not affect the quantity of land he is likely to hold.

Before discussing these results, it is necessary to consider whether they are likely to be true for other parish groups. In Table 2, I gave figures showing the composition of five parish groups, of which one (*A*) is Tunda. By applying the chi square test to the distribution of agnates, non-agnatic cognates and non-cognates in these five groups,

1. I give detailed statistical analysis of residence, descent and land-holding in Appendix III. The results are consistent with the general conclusions given here.

we can infer whether the conclusions about Tunda land-holding are likely to apply to these groups. The test shows that inter-variations can safely be attributed to chance (chi squared = 9.19, df = 8, p > .05). Thus, the conclusions apply to all five groups, and it is probable that they apply to all north central Tari.

In the last chapter, I questioned the significance of the high proportion of agnatic members in Huli parish groups. The data presented in this chapter provide a possible explanation. I have shown that among parish members, more agnates are land-holders that non-land-holders, and that among parish-land-holders, agnates hold twice as much land as non-agnatic cognates. Thus, a man has an incentive to make use of agnatic descent for parish membership. Yet the incentive is not a strong one, for if it were, so many agnatic members would not totally neglect their rights in parish land. In my view, the abundance and productivity of arable land explain why the incentive operates to such a limited degree. Every man has rights in several parish-territories, and I show in Chapter V that it is to his advantage to make use of his many descent ties.

CHAPTER IV

MARRIAGE AND THE FAMILY

A. Marriage Rates

Most Huli men and nearly all women marry at some time during their lives. Of those who never marry, some are physical or mental misfits, while others, in the case of men, are leaders of the bachelors' associations and obliged by their position to remain single. Few people remain unmarried from personal choice.

TABLE 8. MARITAL STATUS OF HULI MEN

Age group	Single	\multicolumn{7}{c}{Number of wedded men by number of extant wives}	Total
		0	1	2	3	4	5	6	
20-25	32	2	2	—	—	—	—	—	36
26-35	15	3	73	22	3	—	1	—	117
36-45	6	3	48	16	10	6	1	—	90
46-55	5	8	28	8	1	2	—	1	53
56 +	3	4	8	2	3	—	—	—	20
Total	61	20	159	48	17	8	2	1	316

In a sample of 316 men, 19.3 per cent are single, though more than half of this percentage have not reached the age of marriage—about 25 years; 6.3 per cent have been wed, but at present have no wives;

50.4 per cent have one wife; and 24 per cent have two or more wives. The 235 currently married men have a total of 354 wives, an average of 1.50 wives per man. The 76 polygynists have 195 wives, giving a mean value of 2.56 wives per man.

Although I could not obtain marriage data directly from women, I estimate (on the basis of genealogies and information given by men) that only about 3 per cent of women remain single throughout their lives.

Polygyny among the Huli cannot be attributed to a marked disproportion of women to men. The sex ratio for live-born children is 51 males to 49 females (in a sample of 250 cases), and there is no evidence of male or female infanticide. The greater number of male deaths resulting from war is probably balanced by deaths of women in childbirth and from diseases peculiar to women.

The composition of the Huli marriage pool facilitates polygyny: eligible women include all girls over the age of about 15, whereas men are considered too young to marry before they are about 25 years old. At any given time, nearly 13 per cent of men are single and have no interest in marrying; by comparison only about 3 per cent of women are spinsters by choice. Thus more women than men contract marriages, and so some men take several wives.

Few men become polygynists before the age of 30, and most polygynists are middle-aged, between the ages of 35 and 50. It is during this period that a man's power, prestige and wealth are greatest. He can afford the bride price for a second wife, and he needs more than one wife to care for his gardens and pigs.

Few men ever wed more than five or six times, and many of their unions are not extant. To my knowledge, the man who had contracted the greatest number of marriages was about 50 years old, a former war leader, and by Huli standards, a wealthy and important man. Over two decades he had married twenty-one times. Six of his unions were extant, seven terminated by deaths of wives and eight ended in divorce. The greatest number of marriages by a woman was nine. A notorious adultress, she was married at the time of my fieldwork—seven of her previous marriages ended in divorce and one by the death of her husband.

B. Marriage Choices

The selection of a spouse is not subject to any prescriptive or preferential rules. Instead, the Huli have restrictive rules and traditions that limit the choice of marriage partners to persons not included in certain categories. These restrictions can be ranged along a continuum, based on the frequency of their observance. At one end are rules that are apparently always observed, while at the other are those which are frequently broken. The former are backed by a supernatural sanction, whereas breaches of the latter involve no penalty or punishment, except mild public disapproval.

Although the rules are apparently complex, they can all be shown to derive from two principles, which sometimes apply simultaneously. The first principle is agnatic exogamy. The second is that close cognates should not marry.

The rule of exogamy applies to all the known agnatic descendants from a parish founder, whether or not they are members of the one parish. The application of this rule is facilitated by the custom of using patronymic surnames. These are not identical with parish names, but they usually relate to some special event in parish history, or to some landmark on parish territory.

Agnates alone are entitled to use the agnatic patronymic. Other parish members, including quasi-agnates, use their own patronymics, whether or not they happen also to be members of their own agnatic parishes. People employ the patronymics as surnames in everyday speech. A visitor from a distant locality is addressed simply by his agnatic surname. Men with the same personal name are distinguished by their surnames, particularly on ritual occasions when pork is distributed. Thus, no matter where a person lives, there is no uncertainty about who is an agnate, and the rule of agnatic exogamy is unambiguous.

In the several hundred marriages recorded, no breach of agnatic exogamy was observed, and no informant could remember one. A breach of agnatic exogamy courts supernatural danger, for it is believed that the children of offenders will die. The practical consequences of a breach also sanction conformity to the rule. A child of such a union would be related to the same parish through both parents and, consequently, would have to enact contradictory roles in certain other contexts discussed later in this chapter.

The second marriage restriction, that close cognates should not marry, does not explicitly define the range of cognates that the rule covers. Cognates who belong to the same parish-section are clearly included in the rule, but does it apply also to cognates descended from a section founder who are not section members? This question cannot be answered unequivocally. Some men express one opinion; others offer another, adding qualifications and provisos. Thus, men assert that a male agnate should not wed a female non-agnatic cognate if both are descended from the one section founder. It is a lesser breach if the bride is an agnate and the groom a non-agnatic cognate, for their children in any case would be non-agnatic cognates through both parents, and therefore would not be subject to the conflicting entailments of two roles in ritual. Yet there would be strong opposition to such a match by both of the families concerned. A man intent on such a marriage would have to pay a higher bride price, and his kin would be unlikely to help him. In fact, such marriages are rare. More often marriages occur in which the bride and groom are both non-agnatic cognates descended from the same parish section founder. A marriage would not be sanctioned if both bride and groom lived on the same territory and behaved as siblings; the marriage could occur if one or both are not members of the parish section of reference. Marriages in this category are infrequent and the groom pays a premium of several additional pigs.

As cognatic relationship is traced through more and more remote ancestors, the frequency of intermarriage increases. There is still feeling that a male agnate should not marry a female non-agnatic cognate belonging to the same parish, but the payment of extra pigs in bride price is considered sufficient indemnity for the shame felt by the bride's family. Two non-agnatic cognates belonging to the same parish may marry without a premium bride price.

It is difficult to discover the actual frequencies of marriage between cognates of varying degrees of genealogical closeness. Men tend to conceal this information from shame. But it is probably safe to say that people who trace or acknowledge any relationship by cognatic descent from a parish founder marry in less than 15 per cent of cases. If the range of known cognatic relationships were extended, this figure undoubtedly would be greater.

By an extension of the rule that cognates should not marry, any member of a father's sister's husband's section is a prohibited marriage partner. This restriction is not applied bilaterally, however and a person may wed a member of his mother's sister's husband's parish section provided they are not descended from a common grandparent. I interpret this lack of symmetrical restriction to the fact that it is more important not to marry a relative of a female agnate than a relative of a female non-agnatic cognate. Huli have no explicit reason for the prohibition, but it seems reasonable in view of the stress on agnatic exogamy. Similarly, a man may not wed into his father's father's sister's husband's parish section, or that of his father's father's father's sister's husband's. Beyond the fourth ascending generation, relationships through female agnates are less important, and provided no actual kinship relationship has existed between a couple, there is no strong opposition to their marriage.

Simultaneous application of both principles of restriction defines a range of relationships in which marriage is prohibited and people are in theory kin. This range differs for everyone except siblings.

It should be emphasized that every person has agnatic status or identity whether or not he (or she) maintains any social relationship with his (or her) agnatic parish. A man is an agnate in relation to one specific parish only; he is, by cognatic descent, affiliated with many other parish groups as a non-agnatic cognate. Thus, agnation provides one clear-cut principle for classifying persons no matter how many other cognatic relationships they make use of from time to time. In this light, the stress on agnatic exogamy and the advantage that agnates enjoy in acquiring parish land seem reasonable.

Certain persons are undesirable as marriage partners for reasons other than genealogically-based marriage restrictions. A man will not wed a close kinswoman of a person who has killed one of his kinsmen, unless the killing has been avenged. A woman who has passed menopause is undesirable because men believe that if they copulate with her they will die.

Therefore, marriage partners are preferred who are unrelated and who are not members of enemy groups. A girl reputed to be modest, hard-working and obedient is favoured over one who is promiscuous, slothful and wilful. Most men consider it a disadvantage to wed a girl from a parish renowned for its strength and fighting capacity. Such a marriage will involve the husband in contributions to his affines for their war indemnity payments and in frequent donations to their rituals. In any quarrel with his wife, the man will also be in a weak position. An important man, however, may welcome such a union in order to demonstrate his own strength and enhance his own position.

A girl who is notoriously promiscuous sometimes has difficulty in marrying, and her family may have to accept a smaller bride price than would otherwise be the case. Most girls prefer young husbands who have no other wives, whereas an older married women may urge her husband to take a young wife to share in the garden work and help with the pigs.

C. INITIATING MARRIAGE

Young men begin to think of marrying when signs of their physical maturity appear; these include the quality and 'firmness' of the skin, abundant body hair and growth of a heavy beard. When these signs are evident, the men resign from the bachelor societies, don the crescent-shaped wig and evince an interest in attractive girls. They do not attend courting parties; these are the prerogative of married men.

Young men approach courtship hesitantly. This is not surprising, because they are taught in initiation rites and in the bachelor societies that contact with women is dangerous. From about the age of 13, boys cannot eat food cooked or handled by women. They are told that menstruating women emit 'poison' and are warned that any sexual contact with females will endanger their growth and impair their health.

A man acquires a wife by four methods: betrothal, arrangement, widow inheritance or gift. The first two methods each account for about 45 per cent of all marriages, widow inheritance for about 7 per cent and wife gift 3 per cent.

Acquaintances that lead to betrothal and marriage often begin casually or accidentally. A chance meeting in a garden or on a path may arouse the first mutual interest, which grows stronger after a number of meetings. The young man may then offer the girl a small present of pork or red face paint. If she accepts, she signifies her interest, without committing herself. The next step is for the young man to find out if there are any obstacles to their marriage. He must learn her identity and ascertain whether she is related to him, or whether any of her close relatives are current enemies of his. These enquiries are usually made in a roundabout way through intermediaries; the young man is ashamed to ask the girl such direct questions.

If no barriers to marriage are revealed, he may make the girl a substantial present, such as a rope of cowrie shells or a pearlshell neckpiece. The couple then begin to address each other as 'betrothed' *(lawini)*. There is no formal engagement, and either may break the relationship without offering explanation or compensation. In fact this happens fairly often.

If matters proceed smoothly, the suitor declares his intentions to the girl's parents through an intermediary; again he is ashamed to approach them directly. If they consent to the marriage, and the girl is willing, the question of bride price is discussed. Once terms are agreed on and the payment is assembled, the wedding may take place. During the interval between the agreement and the wedding, the girl may care for the pigs of her betrothed. This is a reliable indication that the wedding will ensue.

A girl may hasten her own wedding by going to the house of her betrothed's mother and asking to stay there. If she does this, it is a sign of love that no man can ignore, and pride demands that he assemble the bride price quickly. In these circumstances, the man can expect assistance from his parish mates, for the girl's action is taken as a challenge by the groom's close kinsmen.

Before marriage, the lovers are unlikely to have sexual intercourse. A single man fears coitus without the magical preparation that is available only to married men.

Married men follow a different pattern of courtship. Prospective brides are often met for the first time at courting parties which are held whenever a pig is sacrificed to propitiate the ghosts. Heralded by the men's yodelling, the gathering assembles at dusk beneath a rough shelter. A typical party is attended by 30 to 40 married men, and 20 to 30 young girls and widows. Married women are strictly forbidden. The men who come to the party live nearby, generally from several parish groups. The sisters of these men may not attend, as their participation would shame their brothers. Most girls are from parish-territories some distance away. Because of the wide range of kin ties recognized by the Huli, some of the girls and women who attend are bound to be related to some of the men present. These men must avoid serenading them directly.

During the evening the men sing traditional rounds and give choice pieces of pork to their favourites. Between breaks in the singing, the news of the day is discussed. There is no formal sequence of events. People come and go at will, but few stay past midnight. A man may try to arrange an assignation at the party, as most of the girls and women are eligible marriage partners. Once a couple have met at a courting party, the procedure for initiating marriage is the same as that for single men.

Marriage may be arranged by a girl's close relatives. If a girl reaches marriageable age without attracting a suitor, her parents may make a match for her. The girl's consent is usually obtained, for it is considered foolish to force a girl to marry; the union would probably end in divorce, or the girl might suicide. There are enough suicides among women to justify this view.

Sister-exchange is a type of arranged marriage. A man gives his sister to another and receives the latter's sister in return. Each groom pays bride price, but the amount is less than the usual payment. Sister-exchange has the disadvantage that if one union ends in divorce, the divorced man will demand the return of his sister. Men who contract exchange marriages are usually firm friends.

Gift marriages are never first marriages for the woman. In the two instances I recorded, the woman was attracted soon after marriage to a man who was a close kinsman of her husband. As the man had contributed substantially to the bride price for the woman, the husband decided to give her to him. Since the bride's kin had received an acceptable bride price, and the woman was happy, they made no objections.

A widow may be inherited by one of the close kinsmen of the late husband who has contributed to her bride price, but only with her consent.

Young men and men who are shy or unattractive more often

marry by arrangement than by betrothal. Older men and men of high status more often wed by betrothal. Men who wed by arrangement are more likely to receive help with bride price.

D. Bride Price

The term 'bride price' accurately describes the payment made by the groom and his relatives to the bride's relatives at marriage.[1] It is the only marriage payment, for no dowry accompanies the bride. The payment of bride price initiates and legitimizes marriage, establishes the parenthood of children born of the union, and transfers certain rights in the bride from her family to the groom. The people conceive bride price to be an indemnity to the bride's kin for removing her from their territory and control.

The rights acquired by the groom include the right to determine the bride's place of residence (and the duty to provide her with a house); the right of exclusive sexual access (and the duty to make appropriate magical preparations before consummation); the right as pater to any children of the union (the father's right is superior to the mother's in divorce); and the right to the bride's services in child-rearing, gardening and pig-raising.

The wife is not obliged to perform domestic services for her husband; she does not harvest his crops or prepare or cook his food; she does no work in the men's house. She has the right to sexual intercourse, but no monopoly of her husband's attentions.

The amount of bride price is determined by negotiation between the families of bride and groom. The groom takes no part in the discussion; to do so would cause him great shame. The traditional bride price for a spinster is 15 items, most of which are pigs. If the bride is a widow or divorcee, the amount of bride price depends on a number of factors. If she has borne one child, a deduction of one or two pigs will be made. If she has borne three or four children, a deduction of eight or ten pigs is made, as she is likely to bear only one or two children more. If a divorcee is still young and in good health, only a small deduction will be made. If the groom has wives and children, he pays a lower bride price than a single man. It is more important for a man to establish a family than to enlarge it. Competition for a girl results in higher bride price—four or five additional items are likely to be offered. Should a man wed a kinswoman, he pays an extra amount of bride price as an indemnity for the shame

---

1. For a discussion of the usage of 'bride price' see Gray's summary and criticism of the literature, 1960.

of the bride's family. When a man of high status marries, he may voluntarily present three or four extra pigs to enhance his own status. Because of the greater supply of pigs in south Tari, bride price in this area is usually 21 or 22 pigs.

The value of a bride price is not measured only by the number of items, but also by the particular items included, and their relative scarcity at the time. A bride price of 13 pigs including 5 breeding sows, is of greater value than one of 16 pigs including 2 breeding sows. A typical bride price for a spinster consists of 15 items including 3 sows and 1 large gilt. These four large pigs are called 'pigs for the posts'—the marriage is said to be built on them. Occasionally a girl will go to live with her betrothed before the 'pigs for the posts' have been paid; this association may be approved by her parents, but the relationship is not legal marriage. If an instalment of bride price omits the 'pigs for the posts', no legitimate union is established. While part of her bride price is unpaid, a wife feels that her position has not been properly established. She may quarrel with her husband about the deficit, for she feels shame meeting anyone entitled to a portion of it. A husband's failure to meet this obligation will cause marital discord for years, and a wife may take it as an excuse to commit adultery, neglect her duties, or wilfully disobey her husband.

Other considerations affecting the amount of bride price are the reputation of the bride, any existing obligations between the families of the bride and groom, and the scarcity of pigs at the time. A large bride price is paid for a girl known to be modest, obedient and hard-working; a small one for a bride reputed to be promiscuous, lazy or self-willed. When pigs are scarce—after an epidemic—their value increases, and a smaller number is acceptable for the payment.

Other things may be substituted for a few pigs of the bride price; a pearlshell, or rope of cowrie shell, or until recently a good quality stone axe. Before European contact two or three substitutes were the maximum number. Now people tend to accept more.

The groom supplies most of the items for his own bride price. In a sample of 18 bride price payments, a total of 2,185 items were paid, of which 36.8 per cent were contributed by the groom. Grooms received 285 contributions from 178 people, giving a mean value of 1.6 items per contributor. The modal contribution was 1 item, and few people gave more than 3.

TABLE 9. CONTRIBUTORS TO BRIDE PRICE

Relationship of contributor to groom	Number of contributors	Per cent
Elementary family:		
Father	4	
Mother	1	
Brother	40	
Sister	1	
Son	4	
Sub-total	50	28.1
Paternal kin:		
Close	36	
Distant	11	
Sub-total	47	26.4
Maternal kin:		
Close	54	
Distant	6	
Sub-total	60	33.7
Affines:		
Direct	11	
Indirect	10	
Sub-total	21	11.8
Total	178	100.0

Nearly 90 per cent of contributors are cognates of the groom; the other contributors are affines. 28 per cent of contributors belong to the groom's elementary family. This percentage does not differ significantly from the percentage donated by paternal kin (26.4 per cent) and maternal kin (33.9 per cent) (chi squared = 1.74, df = 2, $p > .05$). Of the elementary family, brothers are the most frequent contributors; in fact, a brother often provides one of the 'pigs for the posts'. The small number of fathers who contribute is due to the fact that few men of marriageable age have fathers who are still alive. A son may contribute to his father's payment for a new bride. The point to be stressed is that bride price contributors are bilateral kin of the groom; most of them are close relatives, and equal contributions are made by paternal and maternal kin.

Although they prefer full payment of bride price at the wedding, the bride's family sometimes accepts an initial payment with instalments over several years. The initial instalment must include an agreed number of 'pigs for the posts' in order to legitimize the union.

Neither the contributors to bride price nor the groom has a voice in its distribution. This is entirely the concern of the bride's relatives. If the bride's parents are alive, they distribute the payment together. If her father is dead, the bride's mother and brother make the allocation. If a bride has no brother, her closest male relative and her mother apportion distribution. Should there be no senior member of her elementary family alive, the bride and her closest kinsmen distribute it.

The people say that ideally 10 pigs should be given to the bride's 'patri-kin' and 5 to her 'matri-kin'. They define 'patri-kin' as the bride's father, brothers, sisters and other patri-lateral kin, and 'matri-kin' as her mother, mother's brother and other matri-lateral relatives. These Huli categories are not satisfactory for sociological analysis, for siblings are both paternal and maternal kin. Thus, in describing the recipients of bride price, members of the bride's elementary family will be distinguished from paternal and maternal kin.

Considerations other than kinship affect the distribution. Any person (whether kin or not) who gave the bride a pearlshell or cowrie shell necklace before the wedding, is entitled to a share of the bride price. A person with a claim against the parents or siblings of the bride will try to raise the issue at the wedding, in hope of obtaining payment from the bride price. The bride's family sometimes kills a pig to celebrate the wedding. This is called the 'pig of the wedding' *(nogo wariabu)*, and is usually a large gilt. It may come from the share of the 'patri-kin' or 'matri-kin'. The cooked pork is apportioned to certain relatives of the bride only. It cannot be consumed by any member of her elementary family, or by her true uncles on either side, for this would be equivalent to 'eating the bride's vulva'. The people do not explain the symbolism further, but if anyone breaks the rule it is believed that he will become deaf. Only certain parish members of the bride can eat the 'pig of the wedding'. Excluding her elementary family and uncles, the following rule applies: if the bride is an agnate or quasi-agnate, only non-agnatic cognates consume it; if she is a non-agnatic cognate, only agnates and quasi-agnates consume it. Thus, receiving the 'pig of the wedding' distinguishes agnates and quasi-agnates from non-agnatic cognates, but stresses their complementary relationship within the parish.

A 'pig of the wedding' is not killed at every marriage. Whether it is depends on several factors—the availability of pigs at the time, the status of the bride's father, and whether pigs were killed previously for weddings of the bride's sisters.

Table 10 shows the recipients of pigs and other items from 18 bride price payments. In order to take account of the different value of sows, gilts and barrows, weighted totals are also given. These are computed by multiplying the numbers of sows and gilts by three and two respectively, and the barrows and other items by one. This weighting gives an approximation to Huli values.

TABLE 10. RECIPIENTS OF 18 BRIDE PRICE PAYMENTS

Relationship between bride and recipient or other use of share	Sows	Gilts	Barrows	Other items	Total	Weighted value	Per cent
Elementary family:							
Father	9	—	13	—	22	40	
Brother	11	3	14	—	28	53	
Sister	3	1	4	—	8	15	
Mother	5	—	—	—	5	15	
Sub-total	28	4	31	—	63	123	34.1
Paternal kin:							
Close	10	2	48	4	64	86	
Distant	—	—	3	—	3	3	
'Pig of wedding'	—	5	—	—	5	10	
'Bride's skin magic'	—	—	3	—	3	3	
Sub-total	10	7	54	4	75	102	28.0
Maternal kin:							
Close	11	3	46	3	63	88	
Distant	1	—	2	—	3	5	
'Pig of wedding'	—	—	3	—	3	3	
'Bride's skin magic'	—	—	6	—	6	6	
Sub-total	12	3	57	3	75	102	29.5
Affinal:							
Direct	—	—	1	—	1	1	
Indirect	1	—	4	—	5	7	
Sub-total	1	—	5	—	6	8	2.2
Other purposes:							
Sacrifice	—	—	4	—	4	4	
Mortuary rites	—	—	6	—	6	6	
Unknown	—	—	11	—	11	11	
Sub-total	—	—	21	—	21	21	5.7
Totals	51	14	168	7	240	362	100.0

The amounts distributed to the elementary family, paternal relatives and maternal relatives account for over 90 per cent of the total weighted value of the sample. There are no significant differences between the weighted values of the shares received by each of these groups. The pattern of distribution is bilateral, and there is no preference to either side.

E. Establishing a Union

After the bride price is delivered the groom's kinswomen escort the bride to the house where she will live. This is the house of her mother-in-law or of some other woman belonging to her husband's parish.

All this time the groom remains in his house. He takes no active part in the wedding. The newly married couple must stay awake for four days and four nights, and remain out of doors whenever birds are singing, otherwise the union will be barren. On the fifth day they clear a small piece of land for gardening, the bride using a new digging stick—a gift from her husband. The work is carried out in a formal manner, as it is partly a fertility ritual. It is believed that performing this rite promotes the fruitfulness of their union. During the next few months the couple begin magical preparations which are necessary before the marriage is consummated.

The union is consummated from five to nine months after the wedding. Occasionally a longer period will elapse, particularly if the bride's menses have not begun. To delay a long time before commencing intercourse is considered good behaviour. Ideally, one or two garden cycles should be completed before the consummation. Young men, I was told, usually observe this rule; older men are said to be less restrained. Shortly before consummation the groom sacrifices a pig as a final precaution against the danger of female contamination. Before copulating for the first time, the husband pours foul-smelling tree oil on his wife's vulva, for the genitals of a virgin are 'hot' and may damage his penis. Copulation usually takes place during the day and in the bush—never in the men's house.

After consummation the timing of sexual intercourse is ideally dependent on the wife's menstrual cycle. A couple should copulate only for four days of each cycle. The approved days roughly coincide with her period of ovulation. Whether this rule is followed I cannot say, but the social behaviour associated with menstruation does form an observable pattern. During her period, a wife remains in a special hut and prepares food only for herself. She has no contact with her husband and should avoid looking at men and children. After her menses have stopped, a wife sends a leaf to her husband to signify that she is no longer dangerous. The next day she emerges from seclusion, but still must avoid her husband. The following day she may speak to him from a distance, but they should not look at each other. As each day passes, more intimate relations are permitted, until they resume copulating. As the wife's period approaches again, the couple once more restrict their actions.

In the early months of marriage a woman is particularly dangerous as a source of menstrual pollution. Indeed, it is not until she has borne a child that she is considered 'safe' by men of her husband's parish.

Huli believe that four acts of intercourse are necessary for pregnancy. Conception results from the combination of semen with menstrual blood in the womb. A child's flesh originates from semen, its bones from menstrual blood. A pregnant wife must take precautions to prevent the fœtus from 'splitting' to form twins, for they are difficult to feed and seldom survive.

A woman gives birth alone in a small house. If her labour is prolonged, her husband will kill a pig for the deities, and pay a female magician to recite spells. No ceremony marks the birth. The father must not see the infant for three months; should this taboo be broken, the father's blood will turn to water, and he will become ill. A childless woman is addressed by her husband as 'woman'; after she bears a child, her husband addresses her teknonymously or simply by the name of the child.

F. Affinal Relations

The social and emotional adjustments following marriage particularly affect the bride. It is she who comes to live among strangers and must accustom herself to behave properly towards them. Before her husband becomes a father, he seldom meets or visits his affines.

TABLE 11. HULI AFFINAL BEHAVIOUR

Behaviour	Man and his wife's				Woman and her husband's			
	Mo	Fa	Ss	Br	Mo	Fa	Ss	Br
1. Use of personal names								
in address	−	−	−	+	+	+	+	−
in reference	−	−	+	+	+	+	+	+
2. Joking and the use of obscenity	−	+	−	+	+	−	+	−
3. Looking directly at each other	−	+	+	+	+	+	+	+
4. Sitting near each other	−	+	−	+	+	+	+	+

+ Permitted.   − Prohibited.

MARRIAGE AND THE FAMILY

A man observes a wider range of prohibited behaviour towards his affines than a woman does towards hers. He must treat his mother-in-law with great respect. To use her personal name under any conditions is a grave insult, particularly if she is present. This name proscription applies also in the reverse direction, but a breach by a mother-in-law rarely occurs. If a man breaks any rule listed in the Table, it is believed that unless he pays an indemnity his children will die. The tension between a man and his mother-in-law is symbolized in the following custom: when a man approaches a place where he is likely to meet his mother-in-law, he removes the tips of his close-range killing arrows. If this is neglected, it is believed that if he were struck by an arrow the tip would not come out.

A man treats his father-in-law with respect but is less restrained with his brother-in-law. At first he should avoid using obscenities in their presence. This rule is relaxed when he and his wife have a child, and then his father-in-law treats him 'like a son'. A man should not speak familiarly to his sister-in-law. However, he seldom sees her after she has married.

The rules of affinal behaviour for a wife are mainly intended to prevent familiarity with her male affines, particularly her husband's coevals. She addresses all male affines by relationship terms[1] and should avoid speaking with them unless other women are present. There are few restrictions between female affines. Provided that a married woman observes the menstrual taboos and shows a proper concern for her gardens and pigs, her mother-in-law seldom has cause to rebuke her.

Affinal relationships are extended beyond the particular families linked by a marriage tie. A woman treats as affines all the persons whom her husband regards as kin. But his range of affinal recognition is more limited. He addresses by affinal terms all members of his wife's parish section (or sections), but not other members of her parish (or parish groups) unless she has close personal ties with them.

G. FAMILY AND HOUSEHOLD COMPOSITION

An elementary family results from a monogamous union. If a man takes a second wife his family is called here a 'composite' family. This does not imply that a composite family is a domestic or economic unit. This is seldom the case; more often each co-wife with her children lives in a separate house, maintains a separate garden and makes little effort to co-operate with her co-wives except in matters

---

1. Huli kin terms are listed in Appendix IV.

directly affecting their husband. I mentioned that many men profess a desire to have several wives. A man may take a second wife to gain a sexual partner while his first wife is feeding a child, a period of from two to three years when sexual intercourse is forbidden the nursing mother.[1] An important man takes several wives to increase the number of his children, to enhance his status and to acquire caretakers for his pigs.

The older a man becomes the more likely it is that he will be a monogynist. His wives die from sickness, accident or warfare and he finds it difficult to replace them. Once he reaches his fifties, a man is usually content with one wife. Thus from the standpoint of the husband, unions tend to be monogamous for the first few years, polygamous for a decade or two, and monogamous again during the last ten years of his life.

Widows of all ages remarry more often than widowers. An adult woman without a husband has little status; even women past the menopause (who are sexually taboo) are anxious to remarry.

To determine the typical characteristics of Huli families, I studied 112 units, of which 72 are elementary and 40 are composite. The total group consisted of 552 individuals, of which more than half (57.8 per cent) are over the age of fifteen. The mean family size is five members and the mode is four. The families range in size from one to twelve members. Ten families are one generation units, 81 span two and 21 include three generations—typically a man and wife, their children and his mother. The sample includes 91 husbands and 133 wives, a mean of 1.46 wives per husband. Of the husbands, 33 are polygynists; their wives number 75, giving a mean of 2.28 wives per polygynist.

The Huli family never forms a unitary household, though its members sometimes live in close proximity. Men and women live in separate houses. When boys are 7 or 8 years old, they leave their mothers' houses and join their fathers' or elder brothers'. Most girls live with their mothers until they marry.

Huli houses are small, sturdily built and insulated with grass fibre for protection against the cool nights. The materials used in construction include hardwood for the main posts, rough-hewn planks for the side posts and pandanus leaves for the inner and outer walls. The gable roof is thatched with Imperata or Miscanthus grass.

The house is sparsely furnished. It has no floor and the ground is usually covered with chewed sugar cane pith, an excellent breeding place for fleas and other pests. Some people sleep on roughly-made

---

1. This restriction stems from the belief that seminal fluids contaminate the mother's milk, causing the child to become seriously ill. A man is shamed and ridiculed by his kinsmen if his wife becomes pregnant too soon.

MARRIAGE AND THE FAMILY

plank beds; others lie close to the fire on mats of pandanus leaves. There are no tables or chairs. The householder's few possessions not in use—such as extra arrows, string bags and plumes for wig decoration—are stored on top of planks suspended above the fire to prevent sparks from setting the roof alight.

A house is occupied for up to five years. After this period the posts begin to rot and the fleas and roaches multiply to make it unbearable. When its useful life is finished, the house is torn down; the better timber is salvaged for re-use and rotten wood is used for fuel.

Men own most Huli houses, including those occupied by women; the house owner is generally the builder. Very rarely a widow owns her house. The house title may be held by one person or jointly by brothers or other kinsmen. In addition to the owners, the occupants of a house include tenants and guests. A tenant is a person who lives more or less permanently in a house belonging to someone else. He pays no rent but supplies his own food and provides firewood; if he quarrels with the owner he may be told to leave. A guest, on the other hand, is not a jural member of the household; he enjoys hospitality for a short period and is not expected to supply food or fuel.

A sample of 26 units shows the composition of the men's household. There are 54 men (over the age of 15) and 16 boys, an average of 2.7 persons a household. The range in the number of occupants is from one to nine, and the modal value is two. Twenty-one of the houses are owned individually and five are owned jointly. Thirty-nine of the occupants are tenants.

In five of the houses both owners and tenants are agnatic parish members of the same section. In another five instances the owners are agnates of one parish-section, while the tenants are agnates of another. In six houses the owners are agnates and the tenants non-agnatic cognates belonging to a different section of the owner's parish. In ten houses both the owners and tenants are non-agnatic cognates of one section, whereas in four others they are non-agnatic cognates of different parish-sections. Finally, the tenants of four houses owned by non-agnatic cognates are affines or unrelated friends. Thus the relationships among householders vary considerably, and men belonging to different parish-sections often live together. Men choose to live together primarily from personal compatibility and then from closeness of genealogical ties. Membership in a household is rarely a life-long commitment; members come and go at will. Some are multilocal residents while others leave to join other parish groups.

A sample of 19 units shows the composition of the women's household. The sample includes 29 women (over the age of 15) and 33 children of both sexes. The average size of the household is 3.3 persons and the modal value is 3. The range is from two to five persons. Typically, the women's house is occupied by a wife, her young children and a kinswoman of the man who owns it. In three houses in the sample, the only occupants are wives of the house owner. In nine households there are wives and their children. In the remaining four houses, there are wives and children and one or two other persons: in the first a sister of the house owner; in the second his mother; in the third, a sister of the wife occupying the house; and in the fourth, the owner's mother, divorced sister and an orphaned child.

Huli men are domestically independent of their women—virtually all men prepare and cook their own food. Only young boys and senile men would eat food cooked by a woman. Except on festal occasions, when the men cook collectively, the family does not eat together. This is not merely a conventional arrangement—men are afraid to eat food cooked by a woman because of the chance of menstrual pollution. Young men who belong to the bachelors' societies are subject to greater restrictions; they must take care to discard sweet potato peelings only in places where a woman is unlikely to walk. For them, even indirect contact with a woman is dangerous.

Young children of both sexes usually eat meals prepared by their mothers but may also take food cooked by their fathers. After a boy transfers to the men's house, he gradually becomes independent of his mother in domestic matters. By the age of 12 or 13, he no longer eats food cooked by any woman.

Under the father's direction the family gardens as a unit, at least while the children are young. Men do the heavy work—clearing forest, digging ditches and building fences. Women and children clear the undergrowth, prepare the soil and plant the crops. The division of labour is not strict, except for bachelors who accept no help from women. After the crops are planted, a husband divides the plot into male and female portions. Women weed the men's portions but are forbidden to lift their crops.

The care of pigs is a family responsibility. Tended by small children, pigs root in spent gardens or marshy areas. In the late afternoon, a man and his wife feed their pigs on peeled sweet potato. When it is a few months old, a boar is gelded with a sharp stick. In each parish only a few men keep boars for service; the boar's owner receives a pig from each litter that it sires.

There are few specialists or craftsmen among the Huli. Every able-bodied person is capable of producing enough food for his needs with only a moderate expenditure of time and energy. Both sexes make net bags, pubic aprons and shell ornaments. Men make weapons, stone axes and digging sticks. A few commodities are imported from Waga and Ipili, such as native salt and body oil.

H. FAMILY RESIDENTIAL PATTERNS

At marriage, the bride goes to live with a kinswoman of her husband or with the wife of one of his relatives. Usually she leaves her own parish-territory, but occasionally she leaves only her house, taking up residence with a kinswoman somehow connected with her husband. Generally at the start of a marriage, the bride and groom live on the same parish-territory.

After a few years a husband and wife may no longer live together on one parish-territory. A wife may return to live on one of her own parish-territories, or she may alternate between her husband's territory and her own. A husband may also change his place of residence without the accompaniment of his wife. If he is a unilocal resident, he may change to multilocal residence, visiting his wife every few days. Sometimes the wife of a multilocal resident will accompany him on all or part of his journeys, but she may choose to return to her own kin for the periods when he is away.

In order to study the residential pattern of husbands and wives, I examined where 123 couples were living at a particular time. I classified each husband according to his exclusive residence on his own parish-territories, on those of his wife, or whether he lived partly on his own and partly on her territories. Wives are similarly classified, as the following table shows.

TABLE 12. RESIDENCE OF HULI MARRIED COUPLES

Residence of husband on territory of:	Husband only	Wife only	Husband and wife	Other	Total	Per cent
Husband only	77	7	11	2	97	78.9
Wife only	—	7	—	1	8	6.5
Husband and wife	—	3	14	—	17	13.8
Other	1	—	—	—	1	0.8
Total	78	17	25	3	123	100.0
Per cent	63.5	13.8	20.3	2.4	100	

Residence of wife on territory of:

In the table, the columns show the residence of the wife, the rows the residence of the husband. It reads as follows: there are 77 instances where both spouses live exclusively on the territory (or territories) of the husband. There are 7 instances where the husband lives exclusively on his territory and the wife lives exclusively on hers. In 11 cases the husband lives exclusively on his territory and the wife commutes between his and her own. 97 husbands live exclusively on their own territories, but only 78 of their wives follow the same pattern. 17 wives live exclusively on their own territories, but only 8 husbands are exclusively uxori-local.

The table shows clearly the wide range of residential possibilities that are open to husbands and wives. It demonstrates that brides do not sever their social ties with family and kin, and that they continue to make use of these ties for residence many years later.

A still more complicated residential pattern occurs in polygynous marriage. As co-wives often quarrel, they seldom live together in one house. In a sample of 84 sets of co-wives, 50 per cent of the sets live on two or more parish-territories; 41.7 per cent live on the same parish-territory but in different houses, and only 9.3 per cent live together in one house. These figures do not give the complete range: co-wives may be multilocal residents and some of those who live together only do so for brief periods.

Family co-residence can also be studied from the standpoint of siblings. I mentioned that at about the age of eight a boy leaves his mother's house and goes to live with his father and elder brothers in the men's house. Before adolescence a boy is greatly dependent on his father and elder brothers, and accompanies them to the gardens and on their trips, making the acquaintance of many of his cognates as he goes. The adolescent youth acts more independently. He plants a garden of his own, visits various relatives without his parents and may build a sleeping house for himself. Brothers may live together, but if the difference in their ages is great, they are more likely to form different attachments and live in different places; by the time they reach maturity their interests and parish membership diverge to some extent, as the following table shows.

TABLE 13. RESIDENCE OF ADULT BROTHERS

Residence category	Two	Three	Four	Total sets
One parish-territory:				
One house	11	2	—	13
Two houses	31	1	1	33
Three houses	—	3	—	3
Sub-total	*42*	*6*	*1*	*49*

TABLE 13. *Continued*

Two parish-territories:				
Two houses	42	1	—	43
Three houses	—	12	—	12
Sub-total	*42*	*13*	—	*55*
Three parish-territories:				
Three houses	—	3	—	3
Total	*84*	*22*	*1*	*107*

The table shows that 12.1 per cent of the 107 sets of brothers live together in one house; 33.6 per cent live in different houses on the same parish-territory and 54.3 per cent live on two or more parish-territories. Again, the table shows residence at one particular time only; it fails to show the complicating effect of multilocal residence. Some brothers, for example, are bilocal residents on the same parish-territories, but do not co-ordinate their shifts of residence in any consistent way.

The territorial dispersal of brothers does not indicate fraternal hostility or indifference. Brothers living on different parish-territories may be just as amicable and co-operative as brothers who live on the same parish-territory. In fact dispersed residence has an advantage— by living apart brothers maintain land rights in different territories.

Few adult men (less than 10 per cent) have fathers who are still alive. Those who do tend to live in the same house with their fathers, or in a nearby house on the same parish-territory. A senile man is cared for by one or several of his children. An elderly man who is still active visits his children, spending a few months at a time with each. An elderly widow often follows the same pattern, or she may settle permanently with a daughter or, less frequently, with a son.

The wide dispersal of the family, particularly when the children reach adulthood, is an important characteristic of the Huli descent system. The Huli parish is not built on male sibling groups, nor is there necessarily continuity of residence between fathers and sons. Cognatic descent allows a man to select his group memberships and to alter his choices from time to time. It gives brothers the added advantage of asylum in each other's territories.

I. DISSOLUTION OF MARRIAGE BY DEATH

When her husband dies, a widow displays her grief publicly by destroying her banana trees and uprooting her gardens. If the man dies suddenly, or from some unusual cause, it is particularly important for his widow to mourn convincingly, otherwise she is suspected of causing her husband's death by poisoning him or by failing to observe the menstrual taboos. The widow, accompanied by girls and women who live in the vicinity keen for the dead man. She dons a bedraggled grass skirt, a tattered head-net and necklaces of Job's Tears. She daubs her face and body with white clay which is the symbol of grief. Then the mourners set off on a procession of lamentation, wailing and singing mourning songs which publicly announce the death and the funeral arrangements.

If the wife is free of suspicion, the funeral takes place the next day; but if she is not, a diviner is summoned from another parish to examine the remains and determine the responsibility for the death. A quarrelsome woman is likely to be accused of causing her husband's death. No action is taken against her, however, until after the funeral and interment. Then her husband's brother, in the presence of her father and other close kinsmen, publicly accuses her of misbehaviour. If a convincing case is made against the widow, her kinsmen accept responsibility for indemnifying the dead man's parish-section. In fact, this happens rarely.

Following the funeral feast and interment, the widow mourns for at least eight or nine months. She may not remarry during this period; usually she continues to reside in the same place, particularly if there are young children to care for. Jurally, a widow's children belong to her husband, and she has no right to remove them from his parish-territory without the consent of his family or close kin. If a widow leaves her dead husband's parish, her children ought to remain behind. In practice, she is often allowed to retain custody of her young children on the understanding that they will return to the husband's parish later on. The dead man's relatives are particularly concerned about the widow's daughters, for they do not want to risk losing their share of bride price if the girls are removed from their control. When a man dies his children are usually cared for by his brother or other close kin.

A widow may remarry a kinsman of her late husband or an unrelated man. As I have mentioned, with her consent she may be inherited by a kinsman of her late husband who has contributed to her bride price. Her choice of these alternatives does not depend on the presence or absence of children. She is as likely to wed a kinsman of her husband as an unrelated man, as the following table shows.

TABLE 14. REMARRIAGE OF WIDOWS TO KINSMEN OF THEIR LATE HUSBANDS AND OTHER MEN

Relationship of new to late husband	Number of widows		Total	Per cent
	With children	Without children		
Close kinsman	11	2	13	32.5
Distant kinsman	3	—	3	7.5
Unrelated	19	5	24	60.0
Total	33	7	40	100.0

Chi squared (all kinsmen, unrelated) — .32, df = 1, p > 05.

The form of property exchanges that accompany a widow's remarriage depends on a number of factors. True inheritance of widows, which occurs rarely, results in no exchange of property. Occasionally, a dying man may stipulate that a wife must go to a particular man; this is tantamount to a gift *inter vivas*. More often a kinsman of the dead man who marries the widow pays a small bride price to the family or close kinsmen of the deceased. A share of this is given to anyone who contributed to the widow's original bride price. If she remarries a member of her late husband's parish section, the widow's kin are not entitled to any portion of the second bride price. If the remarriage is to a more distant relative of the dead man, the wife's kin may claim a share, though whether they receive it depends on their presence at the bride price transfer, their skill in argument and their ability to back up their claim with force. The amount of bride price given for a widow is largely determined by the same factors that influence the bride price of a spinster or divorcee—her age and health, her reputation for obedience and hard work and her probable reproductive capacity.

TABLE 15. THE AMOUNT OF BRIDE PRICE PAID FOR WIDOWS BY KINSMEN OF THE LATE HUSBAND AND UNRELATED MEN

Relationship of late husband to new husband	Amount of bride price paid			Total	Per cent
	Full	Reduced	None (inherited)		
Close kin	3	5	3	11	32.2
Distant kin	3	1	—	4	11.8
Unrelated man	19	—	—	19	56.0
Total	25	6	3	34	100.0

The reduction of the appropriate value depends on several factors. If the new husband was an intimate companion of the dead man, his survivors may well accept a token payment of one pig. If he was not a close friend, a small reduction is made and one pig is killed and distributed to members of the dead man's parish section. As most widows are middle-aged or elderly, their full bride price value seldom exceeds 6 or 7 items. A reduction of 2 or 3 items is generally made for a new husband who is a kinsman. Unrelated men must pay the full bride price value.

If a widow returns to her own kin before remarrying, they are more likely to receive a portion of her bride price. This is considered to be partly a recognition of their enduring rights in the woman and partly a repayment for their care of her in the interval between marriages.

A widow who does not marry again has three courses open to her. She may remain with her late husband's parish, return to her own parish, or take up residence where a son or daughter is living. A combination of choices is also possible. In a typical case, one elderly widow who continued to cultivate gardens on her late husband's parish-territory, actually lived with a daughter at another parish-territory and frequently visited her three sons living at two other parish-territories for several weeks at a time.

Under certain conditions a widower can recover all or a portion of his bride price. If his wife dies of sickness before consummation of the marriage, he is entitled to the return of full bride price, or provision of another bride. If a wife dies of sickness after consummation but before the birth of children, the husband is entitled to recover all but one or two pigs. If she has borne one or two children, the widower can attempt to recover part of his bride price, but he is not likely to succeed unless he can show that his wife's death is attributable to some action of his wife's relatives. In these circumstances, the largest refund will be two or three pigs. The Huli consider that his possession of the children is a sufficient return for bride price. If the widower has a daughter, his affines are more inclined to make a token repayment to safeguard their claim on her future bride price. If a wife is killed in warfare in which her husband's parish is involved, no bride price is returnable. If a man kills his wife, he loses the right to a refund and also becomes liable for payment of damages to his wife's relatives.

The daughter of a widow or divorcee may be raised by a step-father. Her brothers and other male relatives nevertheless retain rights in her bride price. As 'patri-kin' they are entitled to half of it, while the other half is divided between her 'matri-kin' and her step-father. The step-father seldom gets more than two pigs.

The property exchanges which result from the death of a spouse are influenced by other considerations as well. A man whose wife is killed in war may compensate his late wife's kin if this improves his chance of obtaining a large indemnity from the person responsible for the death. The tendency to distribute payments on the basis of multiple considerations is one of the main sources of conflict in Huli society.

J. Divorce

Divorce is the dissolution of marriage involving the permanent separation of a married couple and the refusal of either spouse, or of both, to acknowledge marital rights and duties. Whoever initiates the divorce, it is generally the wife who changes residence. A *de jure* divorce is one in which the husband and the wife's kinsmen agree on the disposal of the bride price. Unless such an agreement is reached, and until its terms are fulfilled, the divorce is *de facto* only. Many *de facto* divorces are never settled to the satisfaction of those concerned. In some instances, the claim of a divorced husband lapses owing to his inability or unwillingness to force the issue, or because his ex-wife has died. In other instances, an agreement is reached but its terms are not carried out in full.

I have already pointed out that most divorces (89 per cent) occur early in marriage, before the birth of a child. In many cases the marriage is dissolved before consummation or, significantly, immediately after it. A mother is reluctant to leave her husband lest she lose the custody of her children.

Either spouse can initiate a divorce by desertion. A husband may order an erring wife to return to her parents. A woman may send her daughter-in-law away without consulting her son: this happens early in marriage only when the bride misbehaves flagrantly or persistently refuses to co-operate with her mother-in-law. A woman's family may precipitate a divorce by persuading her to desert her husband, even if she has no personal grievance against him. They may want her to wed someone else, or they may be dissatisfied with the bride price.

The initiative in divorce is as likely to come from the wife as from the husband. In a sample of 154 divorces, there was no significant difference between the percentages initiated by husbands (43.5 per cent) and wives (56.5 per cent) (chi squared $= 1.3$, df $= 1$, $p > .05$). Most of the grounds for divorce which are considered valid are listed in the table below.

TABLE 16. THE OSTENSIBLE REASONS WHY HUSBANDS INITIATE DIVORCE

Reason	Frequency	Per cent
Adultery of wife	29	44.0
Failure of wife to observe menstrual taboos	8	12.0
Persistent disobedience	3	4.5
Inadequate gardening and care of pigs	6	9.1
Stealing vegetables from male gardens	3	4.6
Failure of wife's family to behave properly	3	4.6
Temperamental incompatibility	7	10.6
Barrenness	1	1.5
Other reasons	6	9.1
Total	66	100.0

In addition to the above reasons, informants say that it is legitimate for a man to divorce his wife if she refuses to copulate with him, if she repeatedly aborts or miscarries or if she publicly insults him by suggestive or lewd behaviour. A wife's offence, however, does not necessarily lead to divorce.

A man has several ways of disciplining or punishing an erring wife. An adultress may have stinging insects thrust into her vagina; or her husband may tie her to a tree and light a fire under her genitals. He may shoot an arrow into her buttocks, or he may merely beat her severely. The wife's failure to observe menstrual taboos is the commonest source of marital discord.

Although data from women were unobtainable, some idea of the nature of their marital grievances may be inferred from statements made by their husbands.

TABLE 17. THE OSTENSIBLE REASONS WHY WIVES DIVORCE THEIR HUSBANDS (ACCORDING TO THE HUSBANDS)

Reason	Frequency	Per cent
Temperamental incompatibility	55	63.2
Disapproval of husband's behaviour by wife's family	13	14.9
Attraction of wife to another man	8	9.2
Wife's quarrels with mother-in-law	4	4.6
Sexual dissatisfaction	3	3.5
Other reasons	4	4.6
Total	87	100.0

After a marriage of short duration, the property settlement is generally straightforward. If the union has not been consummated and the bride takes action first by deserting the groom, he is entitled to recover the full bride price. If a marriage has been consummated, one or two pigs from the original payment are kept by the wife's kin as an indemnity for 'spoiling' the girl. Whenever possible, the actual pigs that he has given should be returned. The husband then returns to his kinsmen any items contributed to the original payment. It is important to recover the original 'pigs for the posts', or their equivalents, for they are the most valued part of the bride price. If a man can prove his wife guilty of adultery by the testimony of a witness, by strong circumstantial evidence, or by magical tests, he is entitled to an indemnity from her kin of one large pig. An offence by a wife strengthens her husband's claim for return of the full bride price.

When a marriage of long duration is dissolved, the property settlement is complicated. It is rarely possible for the wife's kin to reassemble the original pigs and other items, and they usually postpone repayment until the divorced woman marries again. The presence of children is the most important factor determining the amount of repayment. As the offspring of a union belong to the father, a deduction is made from the bride price for each child, whether or not it is alive. The amount deducted for one child is two or three pigs, including one 'pig for the post'; for two children, five or six pigs are deducted; if there are three or more children, the husband rarely receives any part of the original payment, though he may obtain damages if his ex-wife was at fault. The presence of children does not alone account for a low refund. Consideration is given to the fact that the husband has had the sexual and maternal services of his wife for a long period. A man with a daughter has a better chance of gaining repayment than a man with a son. The former can threaten to withhold the 'matrikin' portion of his daughter's bride price if his ex-wife's family refuse to honour his claim.

A claim for the return of bride price should be lodged only against the divorced women's close kin. A man should not negotiate a property settlement with the new husband of a divorced woman. In fact this rule is broken fairly often, and this leads to conflict and fighting between the ex-husband and his former affines. Sometimes both an ex-husband and an ex-wife's kin are present when she remarries, and they attempt to reach a property settlement before the distribution of the new bride price.[1]

After a divorce a woman seeks another husband, generally from outside the parish of her former spouse. In the marriages of 42 divorced

---

1. See Appendix VI for an account of a bride price dispute.

women, 37 of the husbands were unrelated to the divorced husbands. In the other 5 marriages, the first unions were childless and of short duration; 3 of the divorces had been ostensibly caused by temperamental clashes; the remaining 2 wives became enamoured of other men, one with her husband's brother's son and the other with his classificatory cross-cousin. Neither case, however, resulted in serious conflict between the men concerned. The property settlements were quickly made, and apparently the events produced only temporary friction.

It should be clear that the payment of bride price transfers a corpus of rights from the bride's family to the groom. Yet the bride's family retains residual rights in her person and in her children. If her marriage is dissolved, she returns to the care and control of her family until such time as she remarries. Her first husband is entitled to recover his bride price, less a deduction depending on the circumstances of the dissolution, and the number of children borne of the union. Often there is a difference between the amount in a bride price repayment and the amount paid by the next husband. By virtue of their residual rights in the bride, the bride's family is entitled to the difference.

K. Norms of Marital Experience

Huli norms of marital experience can be seen by studying the marital histories of a sample of 322 husbands and 417 wives. The men contracted a total of 830 marriages, of which 271 ended in *de jure* or *de facto* divorce, and 115 were terminated by the death of a wife. Of the 322 men, 48 per cent were divorced one or more times and nearly 25 per cent were widowed one or more times. By comparison, the 417 women contracted 679 marriages, of which 156 ended in divorce and 111 terminated by the death of a husband. 118 of the women were divorced one or more times, and 93 lost husbands by death. The details of their cumulative experience are given in the following table.

TABLE 18. Norms of Huli Marital Experience

Experience	\multicolumn{9}{c}{Persons, by number of experiences}	Total	Total experiences
	0	1	2	3	4	5	6	7	8		
Men:											
Marriage	—	107	78	64	35	12	14	7	5	322	*830*
Divorce	167	90	39	11	9	4	1	—	1	155	*271*
Death of wife	243	54	18	4	2	1	—	—	—	79	*115*

TABLE 18. *Continued*

Women:											
Marriage	—	238	148	27	11	4	—	—	—	417	*679*
Divorce	299	95	12	8	2	1	—	—	—	118	*156*
Death of husband	324	77	14	2	—	—	—	—	—	93	*111*

Using these figures, divorce ratios may be computed employing Barnes' method.[1] Counting both *de jure* and *de facto* divorces, this method expresses the number of marriages ended in divorce as (1) a percentage of all marriages; (2) as a percentage of all marriages except those ended by death; and (3) as a percentage of all extant marriages.

The results are as follows: in every 100 marriages by men 33 end in divorce. The ratio for women's marriages is 23, but this is not statistically different from the figure obtained for men (chi squared = .7, df = 1, p > .05). Omitting marriages ended by death, 38 of every 100 marriages by men end in divorce, while 28 marriages by women end in the same way. These ratios too are not significantly different (chi squared = 1.2, df = 1, p > .05). Finally, comparing marriages ended by divorce with the number of extant marriages, the result is that for every 100 extant marriages by men, 61 end in divorce. This figure for women's marriages is only 38, a difference that is statistically significant (chi squared = 19.0, df = 1, p > .01). Thus, on the average, Huli men marry more frequently than Huli women, and more marriages by men end in divorce than do marriages by women.

The lack of data about the demographic composition of the population makes a full interpretation of dissolution figures impossible. Nevertheless, several hypotheses may be considered, and the divorce ratios may be related in a general way to a number of structural factors.

I have pointed out that most divorces occur in marriages of short duration, before the birth of children. Many permanent separations could be regarded as annulments rather than as divorces. In these, the marriages were properly legitimized, but the unions were never consummated; the brides did not fulfil their main obligations. Any union is, in effect, a 'trial marriage'. The possibility of divorce is never absent, though the probability decreases as children are born. The point to be stressed is that Huli marriage can be initiated fairly easily and terminated without any great difficulty.

1. BARNES 1949.

The amount of property necessary to initiate a marriage is not large in comparison with other payments such as wergild and ally-compensation. Very few men are barred permanently from marriage by their inability to raise bride price. If the size were a serious obstacle, it seems unlikely that so many men could wed unaided by donations from their kin. I have shown that 86 per cent of the items in a bride price are supplied by the groom. The fact that kinsmen do not substantially assist each other in providing bride price is not typical of Huli economic transactions. Every man in a parish-section contributes to indemnities paid by the group. Many parish members contribute pigs for use in fertility rites and ritual exchanges. The lack of mutual assistance in bride price payments is an unusual economic arrangement. For Huli, marriage is primarily an individual and family concern, and not an enduring connubial relationship between corporate groups.

Among the Huli, individualistic behaviour is not confined to men. Women have considerable opportunities for making important social decisions. I mentioned earlier that a woman may take the initiative in establishing a marriage by offering herself to the mother of the man she wishes to wed. In divorce, a woman is just as likely to desert her husband as she is to be sent away. The family of a separated wife may encourage her to return, but they cannot force her to do so. A bride has a voice in the distribution of her bride price, particularly if her parents are dead. A Huli woman may own pigs and other valuables in her own right, and she may give them away without consulting anyone. By comparison with women from other Highland societies, Huli women enjoy a fairly high status. While a wife cannot compel her husband to treat her fairly, she can escape from an unhappy union without difficulty. In this cognatic society, groups exercise only limited control over the behaviour of individuals. Should one group attempt to restrain a member too strongly, he or she can always turn to another.

Chapter V

COGNATIC DESCENT AND THE INDIVIDUAL

Early in my fieldwork the range of social ties that Huli recognize was made clear to me by a small incident. A man whom I was interviewing sneezed several times. Standing erect he flung out his arm to the east. Nothing happened. He repeated the action, changing the direction of his hand-thrust until finally his elbow produced a slight clicking sound. Huli explained that when a man sneezes, it signifies that one of his kinsmen is in danger and is summoning him. To discover which of his relatives is calling, he performs arm-divination. The clicking noise indicates that a kinsman living in that direction is calling for help. The significance of the incident lay in the assumption that a man has kin living on territories in every direction.

Other chapters have described the composition of the parish in terms of the descent and residence of its members, and the residential patterns of family members. This chapter is concerned with parish membership and residence from the stand-point of the individual. As group membership is not exclusive among the Huli, the individual is an important unit of study. One example will illustrate this. Earlier, I pointed out that seven out of ten parish *members* are multilocal residents. This is not equivalent to saying that seven out of ten *individuals* are multilocal residents, for the number of parish members greatly exceeds the number of individuals. This chapter describes the choices that are open to the individual by virtue of cognatic descent. It also discusses how often a variety of genealogical ties are used for acquiring parish membership, and what factors influence unilocal and multilocal residence.

A. GENEALOGY AND THE INDIVIDUAL

Any man can belong to two or more parish groups at the same time, and the majority of men do so. To accomplish this, a man must fulfil the minimum obligations of membership in each group. He must fight when the group wages war, whether or not he is a resident there at the time. He does not have to participate in every action, but must have good reasons for not fighting, otherwise he loses his membership. While he may be excused from battle, he cannot easily justify failing to contribute to indemnities paid by the group. Indemnities are paid in peacetime and parish members have ample notice, for the payments are publicly discussed for some months beforehand. Failure to contribute to wergild can lead to loss of membership, and a man can no longer rely on the group for assistance when he needs it. Shame at his failing may lead him to leave the group of his own volition. Even if he does not take this step, a violent argument with other members may eventually lead to his expulsion.

A man is also obliged to take part in the major rituals of each of his parish groups. These occur sporadically, at long intervals, and most men willingly meet this obligation. The ritual leaders may call on a member to donate pigs, to perform part of a ceremony or simply to witness the occasion and share in the festivity.

Genealogy is the basis for most parish memberships, and nearly everyone can describe his genealogical ties with many parish groups. Every man knows his own close cognatic ties; as the ties grow more distant, knowledge becomes uncertain and memory begins to fade. Huli provide for the retention of genealogical knowledge by a number of means. Huli men instruct their sons in a fairly systematic way about their forbears. By the age of ten or twelve, most boys understand how genealogical relationships are classified. Their knowledge comes partly from their fathers' instruction and partly from day to day observation, listening to public disputes and attending distributions of bride price and death payments. The son of a wealthy and influential man has a fuller education. He learns the legendary history describing the origin of the parish-founder, his settlement on parish land, the location of his gardens, the trees he planted and the sites of his houses and his grave. He also learns of the important descendants of the founder, especially those from whom parish-sections are descended and take their name.

Huli beliefs about sickness encourage the preservation of genealogy. In their aetiology of disease, female ancestral ghosts *(wali dinini)* attack their descendants, causing sores, boils and some internal disorders. Although a female ghost cannot cause death, she can enlist the help of the deities *(dama)* who can do so. The first step in treating disease is to consult a diviner or medium to determine which ghost is responsible. The diviner nominates the sick person's female ghosts one by one. If the name of an ancestress is unknown, her agnatic patronymic is called instead. The identity of the ghost causing the illness is revealed by a conventional sign (such as the appearance of a black insect), and the patient kills a pig as an offering to the ghost. If the ghost is identified correctly, Huli believe that it will now cease its attack. Genealogical knowledge is particularly important for men with young children, for children are thought to be the special targets of ghosts.

I interviewed 229 men to determine the extent of genealogical knowledge and the ties that people regard as valid qualifications for parish membership. Each man systematically identified every parish to which he considered himself related, whether or not he could trace the genealogical tie step by step. Then he discussed his current and past associations with the parish groups on his list. He stated whether he was or had been a member, whether he ever resided or gardened on its territory, and whether he participated in its rituals or was associated with it in any way. I also recorded affinal parish relationships in the same way. Few men, however, had extensive knowledge of their wives' affiliations. They were certain only of those groups where they themselves were members or had once been members.

Table 19 is compiled from the information given by these men. A few comments will make it clear. The table includes all the parish groups to which the men claimed to be genealogically related. It also includes those affinal parish groups to which the men currently belong or once belonged. I have not included all known affinal parish groups, because affinal membership is a privilege rather than a right. A man visits his wife's kinsmen and takes an interest in their affairs, yet this does not constitute parish membership. He is not a member unless the group accepts him as such and unless he meets the jural obligations which are demanded of a member. I classify cognatic ties as 'activated' and 'potential'. By *activated* I mean a tie currently in use, or formerly used by the individual as a qualification for membership. In contrast, a *potential* tie is one considered by the individual as valid for membership, although he has never made use of it. There are no potential ties listed for non-cognates.

The men in the sample identified 1,739 cognatic ties, an average of 7.6 per man. The minimum number of ties recognised is 3, and the maximum 29. Men with little genealogical knowledge are either men of low social position ('rubbish men', *agali ko*) or men orphaned in early childhood. Men with a broad knowledge are influential and

TABLE 19. NUMBER OF ACTIVATED AND POTENTIAL PARISH TIES OF 229 MEN

	\multicolumn{5}{c}{Number of parish ties}	
	\multicolumn{4}{c}{Activated}		Potential	
Category of parish tie	Current		Former		Sub-total	
	R*	NR**	R	NR		
Agnate	88	51	8	2	149	80	229
Non-agnatic cognates:***							
Mo	40	94	17	3	154	75	229
FaMo	36	70	18	3	127	96	223
MoMo	30	70	21	4	125	90	215
Other	136	213	41	8	398	445	843
Sub-total	242	447	97	18	804	706	1,510
Non-cognates:							
Indirect affine	5	16	8	1	30	—	30
Direct affine	20	6	4	—	30	—	30
Friend	16	11	3	1	31	—	31
Sub-total	41	33	15	2	91	—	91
Total	371	531	120	22	1,044	786	1,830

* Resident Parish Member.
** Non-resident Parish Member.
*** Non-agnatic cognates are classified by the female ancestress that links a man to his patrilineal parish ancestors.

powerful men ('bigmen', *agali timbuni homogo*), for they acquire their status not only because of wealth and fighting ability, but because they use their many descent ties to maintain positions in several groups. Every man in the sample knows his agnatic parish, whether or not he is a member of it. He also knows his mother's agnatic parish. All but six know their FaMo's agnatic parish, and all but fourteen their MoMo's. In addition, most men know of four other parish groups to which they are affiliated by other cognatic ties.

The same group of men were or had been members of 91 other parish groups either as affines or unrelated friends. Counting both cognatic and other ties, the 229 men claim a total of 1,830 affiliations with parish groups, an average of 8 per man. 1,046 or 57.2 per cent of the total are activated ties (that is, ties currently in use or formerly used as a basis for parish membership). 902 ties were at the time in use for parish membership, and 144 had previously been used for membership. Of the 902 current ties, 371 are in use for residential memberships and 531 for non-residential memberships. These figures show clearly the wide range of cognatic and other ties that are available to individuals for parish memberships.

On *a priori* grounds it is plausible that men make use of close cognatic ties more often than distant ones, if we count as close cognatic ties those traced through ancestors in the first and second ascending generations (Fa, Mo, FaMo and MoMo), and as distant ties all other cognatic links. It is possible to test this hypothesis by extracting the figures from Table 19.

TABLE 20. EXPLOITATION OF COGNATIC PARISH TIES BY 229 MEN

	Number of parish ties		
Cognatic tie	Activated	Potential	Total
Close	555	341	896
Distant	398	445	843
Total	953	786	1,739

Chi squared = 64.8, df = 1, p < .01, ø = .19.

The test confirms that close cognatic ties are used for parish membership more often than distant cognatic ties, but the value of the correlation is low. This low value is understandable in view of the way that distant cognatic ties come into use. It is not the case that a man suddenly decides to make use of a distant tie. Rather, a man is born on the parish-territory of such a group; he may be descended from a great-grandfather who resided there uxorilocally, or from a grandparent who settled on maternal parish-territory. Close cognatic ties become distant ties for the son or grandson of this person.

It is interesting to note that among the close cognatic ties, there is an equal probability that any will be exploited for membership (chi squared = 5.15, df = 3, p > .05). This does not imply that all cognatic ties are equally utilised; it only applies to close cognatic ties.

Table 19 shows the preference that men have for making use of their agnatic status. There is a greater likelihood that a man will *make use of* an agnatic tie than any of his other cognatic ties for parish membership (chi squared = 11.3, df = 1, p > .01, ø = .08). There is a greater likelihood that a man will *currently employ* an agnatic tie than any of his other cognatic ties (chi squared = 6.4, df = 1, .02 > p > .01, ø = .26). Finally, there is a greater probability that a man will be a *residential member* of his agnatic parish than of any of his other cognatic parishes (chi squared = 38.6, df = 1, p > .01, ø = .22).

I have shown that agnatic preference can be attributed to two causes: agnates are more likely to be land-holders than non-land-holders, and they are likely to own twice as much land as non-agnatic cognates. Nevertheless, the advantages are not of great importance where arable land is abundant. In fact, 80 out of the 229 men have never become members of their agnatic parish groups—they have sufficient land in other territories.

The figures in Table 19 also indicate a low rate of parish membership 'wastage'. By wastage I mean the current failure of a man to use ties that he previously exploited. Of the 953 activated cognatic ties, only 13.1 per cent were allowed to lapse, and of the 91 activated non-cognatic ties, only 19 per cent were no longer in use. The pattern of parish membership is comparatively stable. A man often changes his place of residence but rarely his parish memberships. Further evidence of this is shown by the fact that over 50 per cent of the non-resident parish members have been resident members in the past. Although a man's ties with his parish may weaken following a change of residence to another parish-territory, he returns periodically to his original parish-territory to participate in rituals and other corporate activities.

It is of interest to compare the data in Table 19 with that in Table 2, which shows parish composition. The data in the two tables were collected differently. In Table 2, I took as parish members those men who, in the consensus of opinion of resident parish members, belonged to the group. Occasionally, informants disagreed about whether some men still belonged to the parish or not, and in support of their opposing views, they pointed to duties that these men had fulfilled or neglected. In classifying parish members, I took the majority opinion as the best approximation to the truth. In Table 19 I collected the data in individual interviews and therefore could not confirm in all cases whether the parish groups in which a man claimed membership actually accepted him. As I am here concerned with relationships as such, it is necessary only to compare the distribution of responses from these two sources.

This test demonstrates that there is ambiguity about who can legitimately be regarded as a parish member. It is not always certain whether a man who claims membership in a parish is actually accepted as a member by the 'group'. In fact there is no sharp dividing line between membership and non-membership. There is, rather, a gradation of statuses. There is little doubt of the status of members whom the majority of the 'group' accept. There is doubt, however, about

TABLE 21. CONSENSUS AND INDIVIDUAL EVALUATIONS
OF PARISH MEMBERSHIP

Basis of evaluation	Residential members	Non-residential members	Total
Consensus*	395	261	656
Individuals**	371	531	902
Total	766	792	1,558

* Data from Table 2. Chi squared = 55.3, df = 1, p < .01, ø = + .19.
** Data from Table 19.

the status of men who intermittently display an interest in parish affairs. Thus, the membership of a Huli parish can only be described approximately.

B. MODE OF RESIDENCE

In the foregoing discussion I did not distinguish between unilocal and multilocal residence, nor did I discuss the incidence of each. In a sample of 321 men, 46.1 per cent reside unilocally and 53.9 per cent reside multilocally. The 173 multilocal residents maintain 413 parish-memberships, an average of 2.4 per man. Of the 173 men, 69.3 per cent are bilocal residents, 23.7 per cent are trilocal residents and the other 7 per cent reside on from four to five parish-territories.

An individual's mode of residence is not permanent. A unilocal resident can easily become a multilocal resident. Many factors influence a person's mode of residence. If his parish-territories are close to each other, he can readily maintain his interests while living on either, but it is essential for him to have two or three residences when his territories are miles apart. The location of a man's gardens may prompt him to maintain two dwellings. Many men of Ambaru parish (whose territory is adjacent to Tunda) cultivate only sweet potato on their own ground because the soil is not suitable for other tubers. Most of them plant taro in the moist soils near the Tagari River, about a day's walk from Ambaru territory, and they find it convenient to be multilocal residents. A man with a large herd of pigs farms them out to several parish-territories to avoid the risk of losing his entire stock in a local epidemic. He resides multilocally to tend them. The need for security is one of the strongest motives for multilocal residence, particularly in the central Tari basin where attack may come from any quarter with little notice. A prudent man maintains two homesteads, preferably some distance apart, on different parish-territories. Finally, multilocal residence allows a man to maintain several parish memberships more efficiently than unilocal residence. It improves his chances of holding land in each parish-territory.

Huli say that age and marital status are not significant in determining mode of residence. They say that men of all ages have good reason for maintaining two households, as have men of all marital statuses. To test the validity of this view, I studied age and marital status in relation to residence in two sample groups. In both instances the result confirms native opinion.[1]

C. Agnation and Cognation

Why Huli distinguish on certain occasions between agnates and non-agnatic cognates is explained to some extent by the advantage that agnates have in land-holding. Yet, this explanation is insufficient, for gaining title to arable land is not a problem in Huli society.

In my view, the discrimination of agnates from other cognates is a means of structuring an essentially cognatic system. Huli find it possible to classify a wide variety of genealogical relationships into a few categories. A man is either an agnate or a non-agnatic cognate in relation to the parish groups to which he is genealogically affiliated. Non-agnatic cognates define their relationships according to the position of the female ancestor who links them to agnatic ancestors of a parish. This is a simpler reckoning than tracing genealogy step by step, and in many social activities a precise knowledge of genealogical relationships is unnecessary. Only on special occasions is the parish-section divided into agnates and non-agnatic cognates, and even then it is their complementary relationship that is stressed. The last chapter described one such occasion. When a female agnate marries, only her non-agnatic cognates may consume the 'pig of the wedding'; when a female non-agnatic cognate weds, only her agnates may eat it. This customary rule distinguishes clearly between agnates and non-agnatic cognates, yet emphasizes their interdependence.

Agnates are distinguished from other cognates in some rituals. The complex rite known as the *Tege* is one example. In the *Tege*, the sponsoring parish-section is represented by two ritual leaders called *uriali*. One must be an agnate and the other a non-agnatic

---

1. The data supporting this are presented in Appendix V.

cognate—preferably a female agnate's son. It is not important that the *uriali* be resident or non-resident parish members. Their status by descent and their membership in the section are what qualify them to represent the group. The *uriali* receive a fee for their services, and this is paid by the parish-section members. The agnatic *uriali* is paid by non-agnatic cognates, and the non-agnatic cognatic *uriali* by agnates. This is the ideal, but if there are few adult agnates in the parish-section, quasi-agnates contribute to the payment and participate in the rites as if they were agnates. If a parish-section has a female apical ancestor, it cannot, by definition, have any true agnates; here quasi-agnates also assume the agnatic role. Whether quasi-agnates are classified for ritual and marriage as agnates or non-agnatic cognates depends on the number of each in the parish-section. If there are few agnates in a group, quasi-agnates behave as agnates and are classed with them; if there are many agnates, quasi-agnates retain their identity as non-agnatic cognates, and behave accordingly.

While Huli separate agnates and non-agnatic cognates at marriage and in the *Tege*, they also assert the over-riding value of common descent. Occasions for demonstrating the division occur rarely. The parish-section is a small group and it is not often that a 'pig-of-the-wedding' is distributed among its members. The *Tege* is performed every few years, and only by sections that can afford it. In everyday activities, the social ties among section members are overshadowed by the individual relationships of members with outside groups. This is inevitable where group membership is non-exclusive.

Chapter VI

CONFLICT

A. Sources of Conflict

Throughout their legendary and remembered past Huli have fought among themselves. According to myth, the black-palm bow was one of the earliest creations. Every youth learns to use the bow and every able-bodied man is expected to actively defend his own interests. People esteem successful warriors; the most admired men are brave and daring. Huli have avenues for settling disputes peacefully, but they prefer to take immediate physical action rather than enter into negotiation.

Huli have no ideal of *lex talionis*. A man tries to inflict a greater injury than that which he has suffered. Moreover, the people who suffer as a result of vengeance do not accept their injuries as just or appropriate; they too seek counter-vengeance, and the chain of conflict is unending. Even men who fight as allies quarrel about the indemnities for casualties. Each conflict, however it may be resolved, breeds new problems.

Though it may not be possible to trace the ultimate origins of conflict, much can be learned by studying personal grievances, for most Huli wars originate not from traditional hostilities between groups[1] but from personal disputes between individuals. Long-standing injuries may prompt an individual to exact vengeance against a particular man, but this does not involve political groups in permanent-

---

1. Compare the Kuma of the Western Highlands. "Traditional enmities . . . are permanent unchanging political relations between particular clan-oriented parishes. Every male member has an equal obligation to maintain and perpetuate hostility towards the traditional enemy seeking opportunities to kill any member of the group he may encounter." REAY 1960:54.

ly hostile relations. Groups that are enemies on one occasion may be allies on another.[1]

Some knowledge of the causes of war can be gained by sampling men's grievances. The following table includes only significant grievances—those for which some definite counter action is intended: vengeance, litigation, sorcery or trial by the Administration magistrate. I classify grievances by type and by the relationship between the victim and the culprit.

TABLE 22. CLASSIFICATION OF ALLEGED INJURIES OF 119 HULI MEN

Grievance	Same parish-section	Same parish: different section	Affine	Non-kin	Total	Per cent
Murder of close relative	1	1	—	6	8	4.2
Failure to pay war injury indemnities	5	33	5	69	112	58.2
Breach of bride price rules	9	4	25	1	39	20.4
Pig theft	1	4	2	5	12	6.3
Land encroachment	—	1	—	10	11	5.7
Failure to pay debts	3	3	—	2	8	4.2
Rape	1	—	—	—	1	.5
Other	1	—	—	—	1	.5
Total	21	46	32	93	192	100.0
Per cent	10.9	24	16.7	48.4	100	

The 119 men report a total of 192 serious grievances. The greatest number reported by one man is nine; only seven men have no injuries to requite. Thus, nearly every man nurses a grievance that can precipitate war. It is difficult to say whether today there are more unresolved conflicts than before the arrival of the Administration. Conflicts certainly took a more violent form before the suppression of warfare, but there is no way of knowing if the incidence has changed.

The relationships between culprit and victim vary with the type of offence. Within the parish-section, the greatest source of conflict

1. BERNDT, writing about societies of the Eastern Highlands makes a similar observation of the district group: "Any one district may be on either friendly or inimical terms with any number of others, but the position is likely to change almost overnight. There is no permanency in such matters, except in the expectation of interaction itself. All districts other than one's own are potential enemies as well as friends." BERNDT 1955:106.

PH. 1 - A diviner peers into the chest cavity of a man who died suddenly, to discover the cause of death.

PH. 2 - A man skillfully teases the last few hairs into place on a ceremonial red wig.

PH. 3 - A young Huli mother; her infant is carried in the net bag suspended from her head.

PH. 4 - A young man adorned for participating in the Tege ritual.

PH. 5 - Gripping their arms, three Huli men listen to the heated discussion of a death compensation claim.

PH. 6 - Huli fathers and sons.

PH. 7 - To accept compensation or to exact vengeance: a man ponders the question.

PH. 8 - An unmarried girl attends a pig feast as part of the Tege ritual.

is the failure to satisfactorily distribute bride price. Between sections of the same parish, it is the failure to make reparations for injuries or for deaths incurred as allies. Failure to make reparations is also the commonest source of tension between men of different parish groups and its incidence here is higher. Between affines (or former affines) the greatest source of friction centres round the delivery or return of bride price.

It is of interest to note the relatively low incidence of land disputes —less than 6 per cent of the total. Of these, the majority are differences of opinion about parish-boundaries, mostly in areas that were not permanently settled before the Administration arrived. Only one dispute is about conflicting claims to a garden title.

B. Murder and Suicide

Huli say that killing in war and murder are different categories of homicide, though some deaths are hard to classify. When a man kills an enemy in public during an argument, war is almost certain to follow; this homicide is regarded as a war death for the purpose of paying damages. If a man intentionally slays a kinsman it is a murder, provided the killing does not take place during war. It is not murder to unintentionally kill a kinsman—nor is it murder to kill a relative in the heat of battle. Murder is a deliberate offence against a kinsman —it strikes at the basic value of kin solidarity. When murder occurs, a brother or close kinsman of the victim may retaliate, but often they do not do so. If a father kills his son for what people consider a reasonable cause (such as stealing food during a period of shortage) no one is likely to retaliate. If a man kills his brother during a quarrel, his parish-section does not necessarily take action, for punishing the murderer also weakens the group.[1] Patricide, however, outrages group sentiments, and I heard of only one case; an adolescent boy killed his father with a bow and arrow for thrashing his younger brother. The father's brother and some other kin pursued the patricide, but he fled to his mother's parish-territory and escaped death only because his maternal uncle hid him.

In the course of fieldwork, I recorded 27 homicides that can be classed unquestionably as murder. The relationships between victim and culprit are fairly uniform. In 22 killings, the murderers are men, and in 5, women. Twenty-one of the victims are women, and 6, men. In no case was a man killed by a woman. Eight murderers killed their own wives—of whom five had been caught in adultery, two had broken

---

1. See SCHAPERA 1955.

menstrual taboos and one had publicly insulted her husband by exposing herself. None of the killings led to war, but in five instances the culprit paid damages to his affines.

On two different occasions, men killed their brothers during a quarrel. One shot his brother for refusing to give him a sow from their sister's bride price; the other for committing adultery with his wife. In the first instance, the parish-section took no action, but feelings were so disturbed that the culprit left the section and took up residence in another territory. In the second, though the loss was greatly lamented, everyone agreed that the killing was justified.

Quarrels between women sometimes end in death. The women's weapon is the sharp-pointed black-palm digging stick. I recorded five incidents between the wives of men belonging to one parish-section. Two deaths resulted from quarrels about gardens damaged by pigs. One wife choked another for trespassing on her garden. Another suspected that her victim had caused her child's illness by failing to observe menstrual taboos. One woman stoned her co-wife to death after an argument about sharing pork. None of the cases precipitated war, but in several instances indemnities were paid.

Huli occasionally commit suicide by hanging. All the suicides I recorded were women. Few people remember men who have taken their own lives. More suicides result from interpersonal conflict than from any other cause. A woman may commit suicide if she is forced into an uncongenial marriage. If her family refuses to sanction a divorce, a woman may take her own life. A husband who is responsible for his wife's suicide cannot recover bride price, and usually he pays an indemnity to the woman's kin. If a girl suicides after a quarrel with her father or a brother, her maternal uncle may attempt to recover damages, contending that he has been deprived of bride price through an action of her parent or sibling.

C. The Conduct of War

Huli distinguish between minor war *(wai emene)* and major war *(wai timbuni)*. A minor war lasts for only a few days, involves up to 200 fighters and concludes with only a few casualties. By comparison, a major war lasts for several months, involves up to 1,000 men and results in many casualties. A minor war can easily develop into a major war. The first few deaths may prompt both sides to seek a truce, but with subsequent deaths and the enlistment of allies this becomes more difficult. Many wars last for a few days only, some for several months, but few last for intermediate periods of time. I summarize some characteristics of both types of war in Table 23.

TABLE 23. SOME CHARACTERISTICS OF HULI WARFARE

	Major wars	Minor wars
Average duration	4 months	2-3 days
Average number of deaths	17	1
Number of warriors involved	200-1,000	10-200
Ostensible Causes:		
1. Revenge for killing	4	10
2. Unpaid indemnities	3	10
3. Pig theft	2	5
4. Adultery	—	3
5. Rape	1	2
6. Land Dispute	—	2
7. Trespass	— 10	1 33
Relationship between initiators:		
1. Same parish: same section	1	6
2. Same parish: other section	1	9
3. Different parish groups	8 10	18 33
Means of Termination:		
1. Mutual agreement	4	16
2. Intervention by neutrals	1	11
3. Disbanding – losers only	1	3
4. Disbanding – both sides	2	1
5. Administration intercession	2 10	2 33
Outcome:		
1. Draw	6	26
2. Victory – Defeat	2	5
3. Suppressed by Administration	2 10	2 33

War requires no elaborate preparation and a man can be ready to fight at short notice. A Huli ordinarily carries a bow and arrows whenever he travels beyond the borders of his own gardens. He also carries a stone (now steel) axe, a bamboo pipe with tobacco and a day's supply of sweet potato.

Many fights break out unexpectedly, but men intent on vengeance make advance arrangements. They send word to friendly allies, discuss when and where to attack, and send the women, children and the pigs to safety. Scouts reconnoiter the enemy territory. Some of the aggressors are bound to have affinal or cognatic ties with the enemy, and they send surreptitious warnings. Before a fight, a man performs rites of protective magic or incants spells to ensure that his arrows will find their target.

The bow is the most important Huli weapon. From about the age of twelve, a boy learns marksmanship and develops skill with the bow by hunting possums and birds. After passing the first stage of initiation, an adolescent receives his first black-palm bow; henceforth he should fight alongside the men.

Bowmen use four kinds of arrows. For long range shooting they employ plain hardwood-tipped arrows; for close fire they select one that is razor sharp with a bamboo tip. To make certain of a kill, a man uses a barbed arrow which cannot be removed by the victim without aggravating the wound. An arrow tipped with cassowary claw is also used for close fighting. A few men use human fingerbones as arrow tips, which they say is an Ipili custom adopted by Huli who have visited them. Huli have no poisoned arrows, but they believe their bespelled arrows to be magically potent.

The maximum range of the bow is about 150 yards, but arrows have little penetrating power at this distance. The maximum effective range is about 50 yards; at this distance a skilled bowman can hit a stationary, man-sized target about three times out of four. In the excitement of a battle, however, few men are capable of this accuracy.

Other Huli weapons include the stabbing-spear, the fighting-pick and the stone axe. The spear is a plain hardwood shaft about eight feet long, sometimes tipped with a cassowary claw. Men who fight with the spear also carry a bark-faced shield; but this is mainly used in defence, being too heavy to carry in attack. The fighting-pick is a somewhat unusual weapon and is only occasionally found among the Huli, the Waga and the Ipili. It consists of a hardwood shaft tipped with a cassowary claw which is hafted to an axe-handle. A man uses the pick in hand-to-hand fighting, grasping an opponent by the wig and puncturing his neck or chest.

In a typical fight, bowmen exchange volleys of arrows at a distance of 50 to 100 yards. As this distance is beyond the bow's effective range, many casualties are in fact accidental. During a skirmish, the warriors insult and abuse each other. There are charges and flanking movements and attempts at infiltration by small groups. Prominent warriors exert some influence in controlling the attack, but they are often disobeyed. In prolonged fights, different men may lead the groups for periods of a few weeks at a time.

There are no permanent battle-grounds, and fighting takes place anywhere in open country, often near the boundaries of parish-territories. The deep drainage ditches, bordered by cane-grass, are used for protection and concealed movement. Tactics are in part determined by the terrain. In the level country which predominates, defensive fighting is difficult. Most fighting occurs during the day; at night, the leaders post guards at strategic points, and the main body retires. At dawn the battle resumes.

In the course of a battle, kinsmen and affines often fight on opposed sides.[1] When this happens they should avoid each other, but if they suddenly meet, they have a recognized method of mutual protection. One runs up to the others, shouting to his fellow warriors: "This is my relative. Don't shoot him." The latter usually respect this request at the time, but they may shoot the relative later.

When a man kills in war, he enters a condition of dangerous contagion. His shooting hand becomes 'heavy', and he must take immediate ritual precaution to protect himself from its 'power' and also from the ghost of his victim. He must eat and drink without using his 'heavy' hand, lest its potence shatter his teeth. Similarly, he may not use this hand to pass things to anyone else; thus he refrains from sharing his pipe with others as he normally would.

A man who kills in war exchanges his bow for another, in order to baffle the victim's vengeful ghost. He stays awake on the first night to repeat spells. The next morning he rubs his body with dew and drinks bespelled water as a magical protection against the ghost. He then plants a magical bog-iris *(podoma)* as additional protection. When he returns to the men's house, he can announce the killing, without directly naming the victim. Boys, in particular, should not be told the identity of a war victim, for they may unwittingly repeat the name and thereby endanger both the killer and themselves.

The whole parish mourns for a person killed in battle. The victim's brothers daub the corpse with red ochre and paint a stylized human figure on the coffin as a reminder to avenge the death.

The ghosts of people killed in war do not share the fate of other ghosts. They go to *Dalugeli*, a place in the sky, where they are believed to exist indefinitely. From time to time the ghost leaves Dalugeli and seeks vengeance. It haunts the place where death occurred but can cause serious harm only if the killer speaks its name.

D. Organization of War

To accurately describe social relationships in war, it is necessary to define a few technical terms and to explain the basic Huli concept of

---

1. This is common in the New Guinea highlands. POSPISIL writes of the Kapauku: "Friends, 'in-laws' relatives and even blood relatives may meet on the battle fields as 'enemies'. To avoid killing one's own maternal uncle, wife's brother or best friend, one fights on the other end of the battle field." 1958:93.

responsibility. I use the term *war-party* to describe a company of men who fight together; the war-party is not an enduring corporate group and it has no formal organization or clearly defined command. In any war its membership cannot be predicted with certainty. It usually consists of the initiator of the fight, his parish-section, and allies from other sections of his parish and from other parish groups. The structure of the war-party is dependent on the jural relationships among these three categories of participants.

The *war-initiator* (*wai tene*—literally 'war source') is a fundamental concept in Huli warfare. In any dispute, the original opponents are potential initiators of war. If their quarrel develops into a fight, they are responsible for indemnifying any injuries or deaths that result. Each initiator is jurally obliged to pay damages for losses on his own side and, in certain circumstances, for losses on the side of the enemy. Whatever the issue in dispute, there are always two initiators. When the Huli allocate responsibility for a war, a person's intention is not necessarily considered. If a man is wrongly accused of stealing and acts in self-defence, he nevertheless becomes an initiator if a fight ensues.

The people often have difficulty in deciding who is responsible for starting a particular war. Men rarely wish to accept the burden of responsibility, and they may point to some antecedent cause, some previous episode for which they are not to blame. Identification of the initiator is often the main topic discussed at public meetings, and if after long testimony and cross-examination no conclusion is reached, the parties to the dispute may swear ritual oaths to prove their innocence. If this fails to establish responsibility, war between the contenders may follow.

The problem of allocating responsibility is illustrated by the following instance. In about 1934, a pig belonging to Pipigi of Tugure (parish)-*Kili* (section) disappeared and was presumed stolen. Pipigi considered the matter and decided, without evidence, that Pape of Tugure-*Pero* was the culprit.

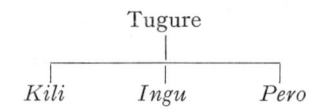

```
            Tugure
    ┌─────────┼─────────┐
   Kili     Ingu      Pero
```

Accordingly, he seized one of Pape's pigs as security *(hebo)* and then called a meeting to discuss the matter. When Pape heard of this he was enraged and attempted, without success, to take a pig belonging to a *Kili* man in retaliation. He was still angry when the meeting assembled and, after a few minutes heated discussion, fired an arrow at Pipigi, missing him. A *Kili* man returned fire and shot Pape dead.

Mongobe of *Ingu* section who had been living in the same house as Pape, then tried to settle the dispute peaceably. But Pape's kin *(Pero)* refused to be placated and attacked the men of *Kili*. *Kili* counter-attacked and also fired at men from *Ingu*. Because Mongobe had resided with Pape, Pipigi held him responsible too. Allies were called in on both sides, and fighting lasted for four days on *Ingu*-territory. Two of *Pero*'s allies received serious wounds.

$$Kili \begin{cases} Ingu \\ Pero \end{cases}$$

Finally, the *Kili* men were defeated and fled to another parish-territory.

After the fight, *Ingu* men unwillingly paid compensation for the two injured allies of *Pero*, although they insisted that *Kili* and *Pero* were the actual initiators and that *Ingu* had only fought as allies of *Pero*. Nevertheless, because the wounded men lived near them, *Ingu* paid the indemnities rather than risk having hostile neighbours. *Ingu* men then occupied *Kili*-territory, biding the time when *Kili* would return and make restitution for the indemnities that they had paid.

In the ensuing twenty-five years, many unsuccessful attempts have been made to settle the issue. Many meetings of the three parish-sections have been held; the Administration Court has been approached but has declined to adjudicate events which took place so long ago. Most recently, *Pero* and *Kili* men have sworn a ritual oath to decide a question of fact relating to a prior and possibly relevant incident.

At present, *Ingu* men state that *Kili* and *Pero* are responsible, because a *Pero* man fired the first arrow at a *Kili* man. *Pero* men assert that Mongobe *(Ingu)* stole the pig and that *Ingu* and *Kili* are the initiators. Pipigi of *Kili* accepts responsibility but wants to make a counter-claim against the other initiator, whoever he may be. The question is still unsettled and is a matter for bitter controversy among those concerned.

I have mentioned that most fights stem from inter-personal conflicts. Ideally, the members of one parish-section should not fight, but as Table 23 shows, occasionally they do so. Often the first casualty in such a fight has a sobering effect; both sides lay down arms to tend the wounded or to mourn the loss. Should an intra-section fight develop into a long and bitter clash, the factions may never reunite. One faction may leave the section permanently, or the group may split, each faction becoming a full section, henceforth to govern its affairs independently.

More often, fights arise between members of different parish-sections, either of the one parish or of different parish groups. When this happens, the initiator's parish-section comes to support him, that is, the members of the section with whom he is living at the time. Kinsmen from his other sections may later come to help him, but their status is that of an ally, not that of the initiator's parish-section. In fact, there is sometimes ambiguity about whether men participate as allies or as members of the initiator's parish-section. It makes little practical difference to the fight, but if they are killed or wounded their status helps to determine how much indemnity is to be paid.

Quarrels within the parish should be settled peaceably, but in fact fighting is just as likely to occur within the parish as between parishes. (Using figures in Table 23, chi squared $= 2.18$, $df = 1$, $p > .05$.) Yet, it is significant that of ten major wars, in only two instances did the initiators belong to the same parish. The most acrimonious fights tend to be between parish groups.

Each initiator is ultimately responsible for war damages suffered by his own side, but he does not make the payments alone. The men of his parish-section (on whose territory he is living at the time) are obliged to assist him. Their responsibility is to him, however, and not directly to the people who claim from him. Consequently, if an initiator flees after a fight, his creditors find it difficult to obtain payment from the remaining members of his parish-section. But, if the initiator is killed in the fight, his parish-section is likely to pay lest his name be dishonoured; his closest co-resident kinsmen assume his responsibility.

I use the term *ally* to mean a man who fights on behalf of the initiator's parish-section although he is not a member. Allies may belong to the initiator's parish, or to other parish groups. They may be kinsmen, affines, neighbours, or unrelated men and are willing to fight even though not jurally obliged to do so. When the initiator belongs simultaneously to several parish groups, only members of the section of which he is a resident member are actually obliged to support him; but, should the fight be prolonged, members of his other parish-sections come to his assistance as allies.

Men of other sections of the initiator's parish are usually the first to respond as allies. They give their help partly on the basis of common parish membership but mainly because of their relationships with members of the initiator's parish-section. They become allies on a personal, rather than on a regional or group basis. This becomes evident when members of two sections of the same parish fight. Members of other sections may help either side; for instance, agnatic members may decide to help one side and then challenge the non-agnates of their section to help the opposite side. During the battle, these section members must avoid injuring each other, but afterwards those who helped the victors boast of their prowess and mock their section members who fought on the losing side. Such a division between agnates and other cognates in warfare is by no means the rule; in accounts of hundreds of actions, I heard of it only twice.

The recruitment of allies depends partly on the location of hostilities. If they live nearby, affines ought to come to each other's assistance, and men who live in the vicinity of the contest may take part to defend their own homes and gardens. When the fighting takes place near a river, the men living on either side of it tend to unite behind each of the initiators. Sometimes men unrelated to the war-initiators respond simply because they enjoy fighting. They are known as 'hot' warriors; initiators welcome their support in the early stage of a fight, but their aggressiveness may become an embarrassment at a later stage when the initiators wish to negotiate a truce.

The number of allies recruited is closely related to the duration of the war. Fighting that lasts for only a few days seldom involves more than 100 men on each side. Of these, about 60 to 70 are allies. A war that lasts for several months may mobilize up to 500 men on each side, that is, about 3 per cent of the total adult male population.

A war may be terminated by mutual agreement, by the disbanding of one or both forces, by the intervention of neutrals, or nowadays, by government intercession. Negotiation may come through a neutral person or through a man with kinship or affinal relations on both sides. Men of high status often undertake the delicate task of mediation. Fights can be concluded in this way only if the deaths are few. It is difficult to negotiate peace if one side has suffered much heavier losses.[1] If the casualties are few, the side anxious to end the fight makes a generous offer to pay indemnities. In this way, initiators may prevent a minor war from expanding and thereby avoid the heavy responsibility of compensating for many deaths.

When both sides inflict the same number of deaths, they do not necessarily exchange any compensation; they may only indemnify their allies. But the parish-sections of the two initiators often exchange 'pigs to bury hostility' *(nogo palia buro)*. Each section gives 30 or 40 pigs to the other, most of which are killed at their separate mortuary feasts.

If there is a marked imbalance in deaths, opponents find it difficult to agree to a truce, for the kin of each victim demand vengeance. They press for a continuation of warfare, even though the initiators want to stop hostilities. Each side keeps a record of its losses on a notched stick; deaths inflicted are tallied against losses incurred.

---

1. POSPISIL reports a similar difficulty among Kapauku: "If the dead are not matched in number, it is almost impossible to conclude peace unless one side is completely beaten or, in very rare cases, the other offers blood money to bring about the necessary balance." 1958:93.

If both initiators belong to the same parish, or if their parish-sections are related by affinal ties, an agreement to end hostilities is more easily reached, but it is difficult to halt fighting in a major war, particularly when there is uncertainty as to who should bear responsibility for indemnities. In a prolonged struggle, shortage of food may eventually force both sides to press for a truce.

Important men of the parish are often called on to settle internal disputes in which they are not personally involved. Sometimes they intervene without invitation, saying that peace within the parish ought to be preserved; they remind the disputants of their common ancestry and stress the danger of outside attack while the parish is divided. They may intervene successfully at the beginning of a fight, but their task becomes harder once allies are involved and several deaths have occurred.

If one side greatly outnumbers the other, the smaller sometimes concludes the war by admitting defeat or by disbanding. The losers may flee as a group, but more often they scatter and take refuge individually with kinsmen, affines or friends. Occasionally, both of the initiator's parish-sections disperse after a major war in the hope of avoiding compensation claims. This is most likely to occur when both the initiators and many members of their parish-sections are killed.

The majority of Huli wars end inconclusively because neither side can summon enough allies to score a decisive victory. The men of a defeated parish-section feel shame and harbour ill feelings for many years; they are quick to seize any opportunity to avenge their defeat.

A full assessment of the human cost of Huli warfare requires demographic knowledge that is not available. It is possible to get some indication of the cost by studying the causes of death reported by informants in genealogical interviews. Of 409 male deaths, 80 are attributed to killings in war or injuries received while fighting. By comparison, 266 male deaths are attributed to sickness, 38 to old age and 25 to accidents. Of 360 female deaths, 22 are attributed to war injuries, 290 to illness, 53 to old age and 58 to other causes. All told, war is directly or indirectly responsible for 13 per cent of deaths.

E. Synopses of War Histories

The discussion so far has centred on the general character of Huli warfare. To show how particular wars were conducted, I give summaries of six war histories.

1. In 1952, two men who belonged to different sections of Tobe parish quarrelled over the ownership of a pandanus tree. They

CONFLICT

grew angry and began to fight. In the brawl which developed, members of their parish-sections came to assist them. Arrows were fired and war had commenced. Some Tobe men of other parish-sections joined the fight, while others tried unsuccessfully to intercede. For two days no casualties occurred, but on the third a Tobe man who did not belong to either initiator's parish-section was fatally wounded. The neutral men of Tobe parish then successfully called for a truce. The following day the whole parish attended the funeral and soon afterwards compensation was paid by both sides to the dead man's kin.

2. In 1954, three wives of Tobe men attended the funeral of a Tombe man to whom they were distantly related. At that time Tombe and Tobe were hostile towards each other, for they had fought on opposing sides in a recent war. As the women returned home, several young men of Tobe berated them for attending the funeral. While they were reviling the women, Kugu of *Wania* section (Tobe parish) arrived and scolded the youths for their behaviour. Kugu's sister's son, Hemugu, who was one of the offenders, was angered by Kugu's words, and shot him in the arm. Kugu called for help, and men of *Yenda* section (with whom he was living at the time) came to his aid. In the fracas a *Yenda* man was wounded. Several participants called for a truce to avert further bloodshed.

3. In 1955, a woman of Tunda parish stole a pig that belonged to Mope of Kore parish. Mope followed her tracks into Tugure territory and met Merabe of Ambaru parish along the way. Assuming Merabe to be the thief, Mope shot him. The men of Tugure, who often fought as allies of Ambaru, attacked Merabe in retaliation. Merabe fled but returned later with men from his own parish-section. A brief and inconclusive fight took place between Tugure and Kore men but, when heavy rain began to fall, they called a truce. At this time people were seriously short of food following a crop failure, and no one was eager to continue the incident.

4. In 1951, a widow of a Halongo man, living on her late husband's parish-territory, had an affair with a man from Pi parish. When the liaison was discovered, Halongo men insisted that the seducer marry the widow. He refused, and the men of Halongo attacked Pi parish. Pi men from several sections repulsed the attack, and a major war began. Fighting continued sporadically for five months, and many people were wounded. Finally, an influential man of Halongo proposed a truce to men of Pi to whom he was affinally related. By that time Halongo had a clear military advantage, so Pi, unable to recruit more

allies, consented. Five Halongo and twelve Pi men died from their wounds.

5. In 1950, damages were paid for a war death to the assembled kin of the dead man. Following normal procedure, the victim's agnatic and his mother's (agnatic) parish-sections should have divided the damages equally and then allocated them to individual recipients. But the men of the agnatic parish-section (*Ano* of Tani parish) took more than their share and departed. This incensed the men of the other parish-section (*Pelupe* of Halongo parish) and the next day they attacked Tani. A major war followed, which lasted for 6 months and resulted in 44 deaths. It ended by mutual consent when both sides were short of food. Today both sides still feel bitter about this dispute, and many deaths have not yet been indemnified.

6. In 1952, a woman of Mareni parish went to collect pandanus nuts in the forest. On the way she met Pongo of Kore parish, whom she tried to entice. Pongo, a ritual leader of the bachelor's society, was pledged to a chaste life, and was greatly insulted by her provocative behaviour. Chagrined at Pongo's refusal, the woman returned to Mareni and asserted that Pongo had raped her. Her husband believed her story and tried to seize one of Pongo's pigs in retaliation. It escaped, however, and returned that night to Pongo's house. The woman's father-in-law, a Mareni man, then demanded the pig from Pongo. Pongo refused the request and fired an arrow at the father-in-law, who ran off to summon help. A battle followed between Mareni and Kore, lasting for only one day, and only one man, Edi, was wounded. Although Edi's own parish-section was not directly involved in the dispute, Mareni was his mother's agnatic parish. He was wounded by a remote classificatory brother. Everyone agreed that this was unfortunate, and each initiator gave Edi two pigs in damages.

F. SORCERY

A Huli who is unable or unwilling to avenge an injury by direct physical action may resort to sorcery, poisoning or ritual cursing. A man employs these methods of retaliation if his enemy belongs to a group stronger than his own, if he lives far away in a hostile area, or is a relative whom he should not fight. He also resorts to this means if he is a coward, or if a diviner has forecast that direct attack will fail.

Some parish groups have two or three sorcerers, others have none at all. As there are no professional sorcerers, a man must become a practitioner himself or else persuade a kinsman who is a sorcerer to act on his behalf. Knowledge of sorcery is not inherited, and those who practise it do not belong to guilds or associations.

Toro sorcery, the commonest form, is believed to be the most effective. The name *Toro* is that of a powerful deity whose power is contained in small black spherical stones that Huli import from Duna. The sorcerer injures his enemies by projecting the power of the *Toro* stones at them.

Only a man who has many injuries to avenge is likely to become a *Toro* sorcerer. The technique is costly to acquire and hazardous to use; the necessary ritual preparation is burdensome and time-consuming. To buy *Toro* stones, a man visits the bi-lingual Huli-Duna area west of the Taragi River, where he consults a local sorcerer with stones to sell. (Huli-Duna sorcerers say that they purchase their *Toro* stones from Duna sorcerers, and as a favour, sell some of them to Huli who cannot speak the Duna language.) Two or three stones, coated with pig fat and red ochre, comprise a set which is kept in a small tightly-woven string bag. Only a sorcerer may open the bag, as it is dangerous for anyone else to see the stones. Generally, the price of *Toro* sorcery is equal to an average Huli bride price—about 15 valuables. One Huli told me that he paid 12 pigs, a rope of cowrie shell, a pearlshell, 2 packages of red ochre and a string bag; in return he received a set of *Toro* stones, the ritual directions *(mana)*, *Toro* spells *(dama pupuwini)* and a bog-iris *(podoma)* believed to have magical properties.

Before selling *Toro* stones the owner demonstrates their potency. He tears a banana leaf into shreds and places the pieces in the net bag with the *Toro* stones. Later, he removes the leaf which has been 'made whole' by the power of the stones. Two Huli sorcerers say they have witnessed this feat.

The newly-taught sorcerer performs the preliminary rites in his own parish-territory. For four months he is forbidden to have sexual intercourse or to harvest sweet potato or sugar cane with his own hands. If he fails to observe these rules, the power of the stones is sapped and at the same time he exposes himself and his neighbours to the anger of the *Toro* deity. After his preparation the sorcerer and a few trusted kinsmen move for eight days to a secluded hut in the forest. They erect a narrow platform about 8 feet long and 6 feet high, and cover the top with *kolama* wood, stripped of its bark. The sorcerer places the stones on one end of the construction and he climbs onto the other. Incanting a spell, he strides the length of the platform. On reaching the stones, he bends to pick them up but stops just short of touching them. He repeats this act three times, but on the last approach he picks them up. Should he fall from the slippery platform during this rite, the stones will kill only two or three people; if he retains his balance, they will have power to kill a dozen.

On the following day the sorcerer ties a pig to a tree and, reciting a spell, shoots at it with an arrow. If the pig dies quickly, the stones will be potent; if it dies slowly they will not. During the next six days similar rites are performed to mobilize the power of the stones. All the tests are ritually prescribed; to omit any of them would impair the strength of the stones and expose the sorcerer and his neighbours to the wrath of *Toro*.

At the conclusion of the preparatory rites, the sorcerer and his parish-section give a *Mali* dance. For several days men and boys perform the dance wearing red ceremonial wigs, their bodies glistening with oil, their faces painted with traditional designs. The sorcerer wears a woven chest band as an emblem of his status. People come from neighbouring parish-territories to watch the dance, which gives public notice that sorcery is in preparation. The sorcerer does not disclose the identity of his intended victims.

After the dance, the sorcerer undergoes further preparation for another four months. He must again observe the ritual taboos on copulating and handling food. With a few followers, he returns to the seclusion of the bush and performs more secret rites. When he finally emerges, people believe that he controls the power of the stones, and they treat him with increased deference and respect.

Sorcerers state that the *Toro* stones emit invisible particles that 'fly like birds' and make a 'buzzing' sound. These emanations can be aimed in any direction, though not accurately enough to kill a specific person. It is said that the lethal particles are not only effective across the width of a parish-territory but may also spill over and kill people in adjacent territories. If a death occurs after a neighbouring group has performed a *Mali* dance, the dead man's kin may attribute it to sorcery.

Toro sorcery may kill by causing sickness, accident, or injury in warfare. If the kin of a dead man suspect sorcery, they consult a diviner who examines the corpse and, after taking magical precautions, cuts open the dead man's chest with a sharp stick to inspect the internal organs. If there are black spots on the lungs, he attributes the death to sorcery. (Several other diagnoses are possible.)

A diagnosis of *Toro* sorcery does not in itself establish the sorcerer's identity. Only another sorcerer can determine this. The victim's kinsmen first kill a pig to ensure their own protection, then employ a trusted sorcerer (not necessarily a relative) to discover the culprit. He cuts a branch from a *waru* tree, holds it at arm's length and slowly turns it in a circle until he feels it 'pull'. The *waru* stick leads him to the house of the man thought to be responsible for the death. The victim's kin may either kill the putative culprit at once, or demand death compensation. When faced with such a claim, an innocent man may admit culpability and pay the appropriate damages in order to affirm his power as a sorcerer.

A war-initiator with heavy obligations to pay compensation usually fears *Toro* sorcery and takes protective measures against it. For a half-side of pork he buys a piece of magical *samubi* wood, which is also said to come from Duna. He cuts it into slivers, which he coats with pig grease and red ochre. He places these at each corner of his house and near the tracks that lead to his gardens. People believe that the *samubi* sticks ward off the lethal *Toro* particles.

Toro sorcerers also divine the causes of death where no foul play is suspected, and they use their power to find lost or stolen pigs. In general, they are regarded as dangerous men and are treated with great respect. A man would not dare to smoke a sorcerer's tobacco pipe, and he converses circumspectly with him to avoid any disagreements.

When a sorcerer takes the credit for a death, his parish-section celebrates by performing a *Mali* dance. A sorcerer keeps a record of his (presumed) successes; he notches one side of a stick for deaths attributed to his power, and the other side for deaths his group has suffered. Huli believe that after a set of *Toro* stones has killed several people, its power gradually wanes. Only an exceptionally potent set can cause more than ten deaths.

Although the performance of *Toro* sorcery is announced by the *Mali* dance, it is unlikely that any of the deaths attributed to it could be explained in psychogenic terms. Most people fear sorcery, but at no time is a specific person publicly nominated as its target. Moreover, the fact that no physical symptoms of illness are invariably associated with sorcery allows people to attribute unusual deaths to a variety of causes. Only a *post-mortem* can 'prove' that sorcery has caused a particular death.

People believe *Toro* sorcery to be the most effective of sorcery methods. It is certainly the most costly. A *Toro* sorcerer who conceals his successes gains little prestige beyond his parish-section. But if he does take public credit he exposes himself at the same time to counter-vengeance or at least to compensation claims by the 'victim's' kin. The *Toro* sorcerer pays dearly to maintain his prestige.

Hambu sorcery is said to originate among the Ipili, and Huli have used it for less than a generation. Huli say that one day two Ipili girls went to draw water at a spring where they heard two large birds talking in a tree. They returned to their houses and told several people what they had heard. On the following day everyone who had listened to their story was dead. When this happened again, the two girls concluded that the story of the talking birds was a powerful spell. They later discovered that, provided they told the story indoors, it caused no harm to the listener, who could then use it too. In this way the spell was transferred from person to person.

At present, a person using *Hambu* sorcery faces the direction in which his enemy lives. He breaks a forked twig as he intones the *Hambu* spell, each break in the twig symbolically 'cracking' a bone in his enemy's body. The victim experiences the full effect of the sorcery three months later. His symptoms are fever alternating with chills, followed by the appearance of boils all over his body. Unless counter-measures are taken quickly, the victim dies within a month.

The antidote is a kind of bog-iris leaf which must be rubbed on the victim's skin as soon as he falls ill. A pig dedicated to the Sun Deity must also be killed. Huli believe *Hambu* sorcery to be effective, though very few know the appropriate spell. Unlike the *Toro* sorcerer, a *Hambu* sorcerer gains no renown. I never heard of a dispute about compensation for *Hambu* sorcery, whereas I recorded many conflicts concerning damages for *Toro* sorcery.

A woman uses blood sorcery to avenge her slain brother. She takes blood from his wound and mixes it with the charcoal with which she adorns her forehead. If the killer or one of his close kinsmen unwittingly attempts to court her, the blood acts as an evil charm and he falls ill. If the culprit looks directly into her eyes, the blood kills him. The woman may also place a drop of the dead man's blood in the spring from which the culprit draws water. When he comes to fill his water-gourd, the blood causes him to fall ill. Another course of vengeance taken by women is to dissect the liver and lungs of a pig killed at the dead man's mourning feast. As this is done, the culprit suffers internal pains and may die.

A man may freely ask a close kinsman for food, particularly on a festal occasion, but the rules of etiquette forbid him to ask it of a distant kinsman or an unrelated man. Should he see another with food which he cannot ask for, he may vent his spite by using *linki* sorcery. Anyone may use this technique, for it requires no spell and little tuition. The envious man has only to swallow his saliva several times causing his soul-vapour to leave his body and enter into the anus of his victim. It passes through the intestines and, when it reaches the stomach, causes vomitting. A man who vomits assumes that *Linki* sorcery has been used against him, and he counteracts it by reciting a spell to make the soul-vapour quit his body. Should the symptoms persist, he makes a propitiatory offering to the deities to elicit their help. Fear of *Linki* sorcery sanctions generosity with food.

G. Poison

A man who wishes to kill secretly may use 'poison'. He may prepare and administer the poison himself or pay someone also to do it. The poison *(tomia)* usually consists of vegetable matter and menstrual blood. (The menstrual blood of a virgin is regarded as particularly potent.) A typical formula consists of a few drops of menstrual blood, sap of the *legabe* tree, the navel of a recently-dead child and the claw of a hawk. The poisoner acquires the blood from his sister or some other kinswoman, making her a gift of pork to ensure her silence. He takes the ingredients to a hiding place in the forest and mixes them on a leaf by the edge of a fire. After several hours of cooking, he places the charred mess in a bamboo container. When administering the poison, he places some on a thin sliver of wood, grasps this between his toes and secretly scrapes a particle onto the victim's food. If this is impossible to do, he smears it on a bamboo knife which the victim uses to prepare his food. If this too is impossible, he sends his victim a gift of poisoned taro or pork.

The poisoner takes a roundabout path to his enemy's house, believing that the route he takes becomes charged with danger for himself and his close kinsmen; should they subsequently pass over the poison trail, serious misfortune befalls them.

After a few days the victim of poisoning becomes feverish and then suffers from chills and internal pains; within two or three months he dies. When a man exhibits these symptoms, his kin call in a diviner (not necessarily of the same parish) to diagnose his illness. If poison is diagnosed, the victim's kin immediately kill a pig. As the pork cooks, the diviner performs taro magic *(ma gamu)*. Intoning a spell, he impales a cooked taro on a stick and scrapes it, letting the shavings fall onto the victim's chest. When the pork is cooked, the sick man eats a small piece with some of the taro shavings and a leaf of the *podoma* plant. The diviner then leads him to the edge of a stream and rubs his body with pig's blood and a variety of leaves presumed to have medicinal qualities. Finally, the stick that skewered the taro is buried at the base of a black-palm tree to ensure that the victim's skin will become strong like the bark of the tree. People believe that, if these measures are taken soon enough, a poison victim may recover, although he remains in danger for a long time. The 'fear of death' does not leave him for several months, the time it takes for newly-planted tobacco to flower.

To detect poisoned food, a man plants at his door a bog-iris called *puri podoma*. If any tainted food enters his house, the plant warns him by attracting fireflies to the door.

A woman can poison a man by seducing him during her menstrual period. People say that during coitus her blood enters his penis and thence his internal organs. Constipation is the first sign that this has happened; later the victim suffers from dysentery. The antidote *(tini gamu)* for menstrual poisoning is an infusion of several kinds of leaves and grasses thought to have therapeutic properties. Men who treat this condition also employ spells and kill pigs if the victim's health deteriorates.

H. Ritual Cursing

A *ritual curse* injures an enemy by calling down the wrath of certain deities on him. Only a few men know the appropriate imprecations, but their services can be hired for a half-side of pork or a rope of cowrie shell.

The client first kills and cooks a pig at a forest shrine dedicated to the nine evil deities in the Huli pantheon. There are three or four such shrines in the central Tari basin, and with the aid of an imprecator anyone may kill pigs at them. The cooked pork is placed in the shrine while the imprecator calls on each of the evil deities. Then he utters the ritual curse which the client repeats, phrase by phrase. Together they ask that the enemy's eyes may become blind, his ears turn deaf, his skin dry up and his penis fall off, or that some grievous harm may befall his family.

Men believe that a curse usually takes effect within eight days of its utterance, and at the most within two months. The client attributes to it any sickness, injury, or misfortune that the enemy or any member of his parish-section suffers during this period.

Reciprocal oath-taking[1] is a form of ritual cursing. When two men dispute a question of fact, such as the responsibility for initiating a war, one may challenge the other to take a ritual oath as a test of his innocence. Public opinion may turn against a man who refuses the challenge. Each of the contestants asserts his own blamelessness and exhorts the deities to harm the liar. As the first man recites the oath he takes a parcel of bespelled pork and smites the other with it on the back; the second man repeats the oath and returns the blow. If any member of the parish-section (of current residence) of either

---

1. HUBER defines a ritual oath as "a way of calling down supernatural sanctions upon a person from whom one has suffered grave injustice". 1959:41.

man suffers misfortune during the next two months, guilt falls on him, and he must pay compensation to his opponent and also to the elementary family of the victim.

I. Ritual Conflict

Cognatic societies such as the Huli are bound to produce a high rate of interpersonal conflict, mainly because group membership is non-exclusive. The parish is not a residential unit even though it owns land, and the majority of residential members spend only part of their time on the group territory. The loyalty of the individual is divided and in a war he often has allegiance to both sides.

It could be argued that the prevalence of cross-cutting ties[1] has an inhibiting effect on the direct expression of conflict, that men attempt to intercede in quarrels when they have attachments to both disputants. But this presumes a calculation that is not characteristic of the Huli. Huli are volatile and quick tempered; they lack deliberation and they swiftly resort to arms. Few men in a crisis pause to weigh their obligations and responsibilities; they take decisions on the basis of current, immediate sympathies, often to find their own brothers on the opposite side.

Not everyone acts so impulsively. Men torn by indecision or by the impropriety of a contemplated action turn to divination as a guide. There are many techniques available and many skilled practitioners to serve them. Divination is a way of externalising difficult choices, and it frees the individual from personal culpability or guilt for the consequences of his behaviour.

Despite the emotional ease which most Huli display in taking decisions, and despite the comfort that comes from externalising choice, there are many occasions when the interests of parish members, and especially parish-section members, diverge. At times these differences lead men to breaking point, and open schism occurs within the group. Huli periodically discharge intra-group tension in ritually prescribed conflict. This ventilating device is a highlight of the *Tege* ritual.

This part of the ritual takes place an hour before dawn. All night the *Tege* sponsors (one, sometimes two parish-sections) stay awake, initiating boys by ordeal and frightening them with bizarre behaviour into submissive acceptance of their status. Two hours before dawn, the ritual leaders stoke up the fires in the long triangular-shaped *Tege* house. The guardians of the initiates stand behind the boys on the

---

1. See Colson 1953.

low platforms that flank the centre aisle where the fires burn. At a signal from the ritual leaders, second stage initiates enter the house at one end, and when the fires have died to glowing coals, they run the length of the centre aisle, avoiding the coals as best they can, while the *Tege* sponsors lash at them with birch switches. Youth after youth runs the ribbon of coals, while the first stage initiates huddle near the exit watching the proceedings. The sponsors of the parish-section act together in whipping the fire-runners. They unite in ritual violence, lashing each youth as he passes.

An hour before dawn the cry of certain birds signals the next phase of the rites. With torches of burning cane for illumination, everyone goes outside. The men of the sponsoring parish-section are all present —residents, non-residents, even men who rarely participate in section activity. One by one a man calls on members against whom he has a grievance to take a birching. He may nominate any one present, except his father or father's brother. The nominee must turn his back and accept the blows. Before striking, the whipper cites a specific act of misbehaviour—failure to contribute to a section indemnity, or a failure to kill pigs at a mortuary feast. He may also condemn the nominee for fighting against him in a war, or for residing away from the parish-territory for too long a period. He may enjoin him to fulfil some neglected duty, to exact vengeance for the death of a kinsman, to respond promptly when the section calls for his help, or to marry a girl from an appropriate category. Then he flays the man across the back two or three times with a birch rod.

The whipped man has the right to reciprocate (except if the striker is his father or paternal uncle). He exercises this right immediately, counter-indicting his attacker for some failing of his own and switching him with equal energy. Several beatings take place simultaneously. Tempers are inflamed. Often the affair flares into a wild free-for-all, the men lashing out at each other with abandon.

During the melee, one ritual leader remains aside, aloof from the excitement, listening for the cry of the *urungawe* bird, which is the signal for whipping to cease. When he hears it he shouts the traditional call of the war-party returning from battle. The men throw down their switches and join in the victory call. Chanting in unison, they circle round the *Tege* house until finally exhausted, they depart for a few hours rest.

This part of the *Tege* effectively releases intra-section hostility. Informants affirm this explicitly. They say that everyone has a 'good feeling' after the brawl, and this is carried over to the pig feast which takes place later in the day.

The switching is violent and painful, but it causes no permanent damage—only the welts which are laughingly displayed. Everyone knows that the beating will last for only an hour, and that when the signal comes they must stop. Given this licence, men freely express their conflicts. They ventilate their personal enmities within the framework of prescribed ritual behaviour, and finally reassert their unity in a victory dance. Ritual conflict is an effective, though temporary solution to the problem of divided allegiance in a cognatic society.[1]

1. REAY (1959) discusses ritual conflicts of a different kind among the Kuma.

Chapter VII

COMPENSATION

Everyone in Huli society is held responsible for the consequences of his or her actions. Only the insane are exempt from this rule, but their kin are responsible for their acts and must pay damages if they cause harm. In determining responsibility, Huli rarely consider a person's motive or intent. They show little concern for extenuating circumstances; it is the consequences of an act that they consider. This ethic leaves little place for the accidental. Events have causes, direct or indirect, and wherever possible Huli try to establish individual responsibility.

Huli believe that direct physical retaliation is the best way to requite a wrong, but they accept compensation as a substitute in many instances. They pay indemnities not only for individual offences, such as murder, theft and adultery, but for the losses and injuries inflicted and received in war.

Huli recognise three classes of indemnity. Private indemnities *(abi)*, which I call *damages*, are payments by a person who offends or injures another by property infraction, sexual offence or breaking a taboo believed to cause injury or shame. War indemnities *(nogo abi)*, which I call *reparations*, are payments made by the initiator of a war for the wounds and deaths of members of his war-party. Enemy indemnities *(nogo timu)*, which I call *wergild*,[1] are paid for enemy losses by the initiator to the victim's kin. Because of the distinction between reparations and wergild, it is possible for one war death to be compensated from two sources; the victim's kin

---

1. RADCLIFFE-BROWN defines wergild in relation to the Teutonic system as "an indemnity for homicide paid to those persons who had possessive rights (rights *in rem*) over the person who was killed . . . These rights were held by the cognatic relatives of the slain man". 1950:17.

are entitled to reparation from the initiator for whom the victim fought, and in certain conditions they may also receive wergild from the victim's slayer.

A. Damages

Property infractions can be settled by the payment of damages. These include theft, trespass and the use of gardens without permission. A thief who is caught must pay back four or five times the value of the stolen object. A person who steals from a garden must repay a string of cowrie shell or a small pig. A man is liable for damages if his pig breaks into a garden and causes destruction. The garden owner may forego damages the first time, provided the pig owner helps him repair the broken fence. If it happens again, however, he seeks damages in proportion to the crop destroyed.

Sexual offences can also be adjusted by compensation. A rapist may escape retaliation by quickly paying damages to the girl's kin. A man who seduces a girl with her consent is also liable for damages; the girl is 'spoiled' for marriage and her brothers not only punish her but demand damages from the man. A cuckold is entitled to damages both from his male affines and from his wife's lover. The adulterer pays two or three pigs, while her family give one or two. If the adulterer is a kinsman, higher damages are claimed. A member of a bachelor's cult group who breaks the rule of chastity exposes the group to supernatural danger, and because of his offence, their magical iris plants will not thrive, their health will deteriorate and their 'skin will not grow'. The group expels the guilty man and he must also pay four or five pigs or risk their vengeance. Huli consider it an offence for a wife to menstruate the day after her marriage is consummated. The quick onset of her menses is thought to endanger her husband's health. The husband divorces her immediately, has his bride price refunded and claims damages of seven or eight pigs. If a wife breaks any other menstrual taboo, her husband is entitled to damages from her father or brother. To succeed in his claim, he must exhibit a skin rash or some other sign of injury. The amount of damages he receives depends on the seriousness of his disorder.

People who utter obscenities may be charged with insult. A man may remark jokingly to another "Eat your mother's menstrual blood" or "Eat your sister's vulva", but if he says this venomously and in public it is an offence. The larger the audience, the graver the insult. The scale of damages is proportionate to the gravity of the insult. A man offends his mother-in-law by speaking her name; he compensates her with a gift of pork for if he fails to do this his children will fall ill.

A single man is offended if someone speaks of coitus or female genitalia in his presence. The offence is particularly serious if he is a member of a bachelors' cult, and he may claim damages of one or two pigs. A woman insults her husband by behaving lewdly or suggestively in public. Her husband claims damages from her parents or brothers after beating her severely.

Murder too can be compounded by damages. As I mentioned, homicide within the parish-section does not necessarily provoke retaliation. It depends on the relationship between the killer and the victim. If the pair are distant kinsmen, the section may split into factions and fight, but the killing of a close kinsman creates a problem. The men whose duty it is to avenge the death are also close relatives of the murderer. In this situation, the killer ought to compensate his section members with seven or eight pigs. If he does this, they in turn will join with him in compensating relatives outside the section. In one instance, Tagube murdered his MoSsSn during an argument about how to divide a small inheritance of cowrie shell from their grandfather. Tagube fled and took up residence on another parish-territory. The incident took place on Tagube's mother's (agnatic) territory, and the paternal kin of the dead man demanded damages from members of Tagube's mother's (agnatic) section. The section disclaimed responsibility, but after an angry discussion, decided to pay eight pigs on Tagube's behalf, which they hope to recover from him. All damage payments are sanctioned by force or threat of war.

B. Preliminaries to War Indemnity

When a person dies from war injuries, people come from near and far to attend the burial. If deaths occur simultaneously on both sides, a truce may be called to hold the funerals, otherwise relatives of the victim carry the body to a safe place while some remain behind to guard against attack. News of the death is yodelled from group to group and the next morning friends and relatives assemble to mourn the loss. The body is laid out on a platform under a rough shelter (*tuganda*, literally 'the house of tears'). Dry-eyed, the men quietly watch the funeral preparations. The women wail and keen, lamenting the loss in song and mournful dance. It is not an occasion for oratory, but a few men gravely extol the dead man's virtues and vow to avenge him. Two days of mourning precede the burial, allowing kinsmen from distant territories to hear the news and come for the final rites.

Burial takes place soon after mid-day on the third day. Two bearers *(homa guini)* carry the body tied to a pole from its resting place to the interment platform;[1] male bearers carry the bodies of men, women bearers those of women and small children.[2] The wailing reaches a climax as the body is interred in a bark coffin and the lid is closed.

That afternoon the mortuary feast is held. Many of the mourners bring pigs *(homa nogo)* for the feast to honour the dead man. This donation entitles them to receive in due course a pig from the reparation payment. Any friend or relative may donate a pig, and usually the father and brothers of the dead man give several.

At the food distribution, a half side of pork is given to each man who touched the body immediately after death. This payment, called *luari*, is an indemnity for the risk they have taken by touching the dead. The donor of a pig used for a *luari* payment is also entitled to share in reparation. The pork[3] is distributed to everyone present. The women and children depart after receiving their share and the men remain and begin to discuss reparations.[4]

If the initiator of the war is present at the feast, he with the aid of close kinsmen pays several half-sides of pork to the dead man's next-of-kin, as an *earnest* of his intention to pay reparation. The payment, which is called *nogo dauhupwa*, shows publicly his acceptance of responsibility to pay damages. The size of the payment depends on the circumstances of the death and the status of the victim. If many deaths occur, the earnest for each is less than for a single death. If a 'big man' dies, a large amount is paid, for many people will partake of it. The earnest is not part of the reparation but only an acknowledgment that it will be paid. The father or brothers of the victim receive the earnest and they distribute it among their bilateral kin, particularly those who have been closely attached to the dead man.

---

1. It is a mark of respect to inter a body on a platform. People who die of a sudden sickness, from leprosy or from 'sorcery' are given earth burials instead. For an illustration of an interment platform similar to that of the Huli, see Figure 5, WILLIAMS 1939:50.
2. In each parish-section there are four bearers, two men and two women. They carry the corpses of all members, save those of their own close relatives, who are carried by bearers from another section. To protect themselves from the danger of contact with the dead, the bearers are covered with white clay and when their task is done they must wash carefully. Each receives a pig or a pearlshell for the work.
3. From 2 to 20 pigs are killed at a funeral feast, the number depending on the availability of pigs at the time, and the status of the dead man. Few pigs are killed for the death of a child, many for an important warrior.
4. A female diviner is called in before burial to determine whether they should avenge the death or seek wergild from the enemy. Alone, late at night, she incants a spell over the corpse. By examining the dead man's penis she can then forecast if vengeance would be successful; if the signs are against it, she advises that wergild should be sought. Wergild and vengeance should not be exacted for the same death. By accepting wergild, a man relinquishes the right to vengeance; by breaking the rule he risks supernatural punishment.

At the presentation of the earnest, the size of the reparation payment is discussed. The initiator should not haggle over the amount, for it is despicable to question the value of a life. A 'good man' *(agali baigeli)* accepts the figure proposed by the next-of-kin, a 'big man' *(agali homogo)* increases it. In deciding how much to demand, the claimant considers several things. If only one man has been slain, he rightfully feels his loss to be great, and asks for a high payment.[1] If many have died, he accepts the general misfortune and asks for a lesser amount. The minimum payment for a single death is 30 valuables, most of which must be pigs. The largest payment I recorded was 150 pigs—in this case the war-initiator was a man of exceptionally high status.

There is often a long delay between the payments of an earnest and the reparation. Ideally, war deaths should be compensated in the order that they occur but this seldom happens. Some claimants can exert pressure in support of their demands, and if the claimant lives near the territory of the initiator he has a good chance of quick payment. It is unwise to alienate a neighbour. Similarly, a renowned fighter has a better chance than an old man.

The initiator is responsible for reparations but does not pay them alone. Members of his parish-section are obliged to assist him, and other kinsmen, affines and friends also contribute. Each section member should contribute at least one pig, while the initiator and his closest kin should provide the breeding sows for the payment. A big-man demonstrates his position by making a large donation. A man unable to contribute is deeply shamed; a man unwilling to donate may lose his section rights.[2]

If the initiator dies while fighting, his responsibility falls to his section mates. They rarely accept it willingly, but the threats of the victim's kin force them to pay.

The relationship between the initiator and the victim largely determines the contributors to reparation payments. Two kinds of relationship are possible. The victim may be an ally of the initiator (either from another section of the initiator's parish or from another parish), or he may be a member of the initiator's parish-section. Of course, it is also possible that the initiator himself falls victim. In a sample of 119 war fatalities, 34 victims are members of other sections of the initiator's parish, 60 are from other parish groups, 16 are

---

1. The Huli counting system is based on 15. Reparations start at 15 and increase by multiples of 15.
2. PETERS makes a similar point about the Bedouin: "The test, par excellence, of corporate affiliation is the acceptance of the responsibility to pay blood-money. Refusal to accept this is the same as renouncing membership of the group. Individuals are sometimes excluded from membership in this way." 1960:47.

members of the initiator's own section and in 9 instances the initiator himself died.[1]

If the victim is a member of the initiator's section, a complex situation arises. It may first be necessary for the initiator to pay intra-section reparations, depending on the degree of his cognatic relationship with the victim. If his father or brother is killed, he pays no internal reparation, for he is the chief sufferer. If the victim is a distant kinsman, other men suffer by the loss more than he does, and internal payment must be made. The initiator again receives donations from his own close kinsmen. Together, they give pigs to the victim's next-of-kin who in turn allots them to his close cognates. The principle that applies in determining whether payment should be made applies again in determining the size of the payment—the nearer the relationship between initiator and victim, the smaller the payment, for the initiator's personal loss is relatively small when a distant kinsman dies. The size of the payment ranges from two to eight pigs.

In intra-section reparation, it is possible for some men to donate one pig to the initiator and receive one from the victim's kin. They give on the basis of one relationship and receive on the basis of another.

Relationships between Donors and Recipients in Intra-Section Reparations

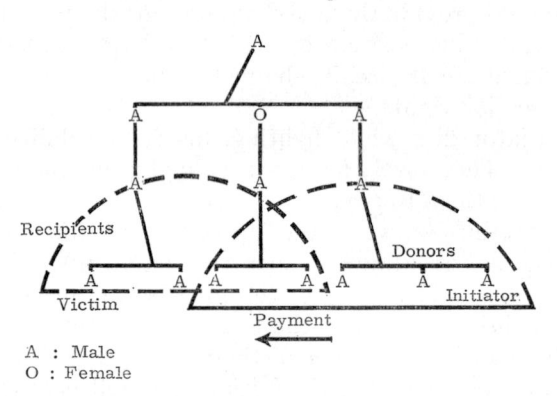

A : Male
O : Female

Other people beside section members have a claim on the initiator for reparations. The initiator receives little support from his section mates in compensating others unless he first settles claims for intra-section reparations. The other claims come from cognatic kin of the

---

1. This distribution shows the importance of allies in war. Few battles are limited to two parish-sections, and 79 per cent of war victims are allies.

victim who are not section members. If the victim dies while fighting for his agnatic parish-section, claims are made not only by matrilateral kin but by kin from his FaMo's (agnatic) section and any other patrilateral kin who were socially important to him. If the victim dies fighting as a member of his mother's (agnatic) parish, in the same way his patrilateral kin and his other matrilateral kin are entitled to reparations.

The amount of the external payment is less than for the death of an ally because the section itself has suffered by the loss. For example, Talube, an agnatic member of *Mataba-Kili* died fighting for his section *(-Kili)*. Where the initiator would have paid 30 pigs to an ally, he paid only 3 pigs in internal reparation. Then *Kili* men pooled together and paid 7 pigs to Talube's FaMo's (agnatic) section, of which Talube was also an active member, and 15 more pigs to matrilateral kin belonging to three different parish groups.

The initiator is also responsible for indemnities for wounds. These, called *nogo nisi*, consist of two or three pigs which go to the injured man. He dedicates and kills them to secure supernatural aid in his convalescence. If his wound heals he has no further claim; if it does not, he can claim up to fifteen pigs from the initiator. If he does not personally receive them, his next-of-kin claim them upon his death.

Many conflicts arise from claims for wound payments. It is often debatable that a particular wound is impairing a man's health. Men receive numerous wounds during the course of their lives, and each contributes to their condition. Because of this, it is difficult to fix responsibility, and men are always more reluctant to pay claims for old wounds than for those of recent origin.

After a major war, a parish-section becomes liable for reparations for up to twenty deaths. Rather than meet each payment jointly, the group often agrees to divide the commitment. The resident agnates pay for a few deaths, the resident non-agnatic cognates elect to pay others, while non-residents collectively compensate the remainder. The division of responsibility need not follow lines of descent or residence Sometimes the single men decide to pay off one claim, the married men another. At other times, the men living in certain houses agree to act together. Usually the 'big men' of a section decide the best way to divide responsibility—they are trusted to make a fair decision.

Table 24 shows the donors to reparations and the value of their contributions in 14 payments. Each division in the table represents a different parish-section. To eliminate bias (owing to the division of commitments) I give composite figures for each of the three parish-sections. In sections A and B, the reparations are for five deaths

TABLE 24. CONTRIBUTIONS TO HULI REPARATIONS

Donors	Sows	Gilts	Barrows	All	Value	No. of Donors
A. Initiator's parish-section:						
Agnates	6	5	34	45	68	7
Non-agnatic cognates	9	12	78	99	129	13
Direct affines	—	—	11	11	11	3
Indirect affines	—	—	13	13	13	3
Sub-total	*15*	*17*	*136*	*168*	*221*	*26*
Initiator's parish – other section:						
Section (i)	—	—	6	6	6	6
Total	*15*	*17*	*142*	*174*	*227*	*32*
B. Initiator's parish-section:						
Agnates	9	13	46	68	99	16
Non-agnatic cognates	11	10	40	61	93	12
Indirect affines	—	—	2	2	2	2
Direct affines	—	—	4	4	4	4
Others	—	—	8	8	8	7
Sub-total	*20*	*23*	*100*	*143*	*206*	*41*
Initiator's parish – other sections:						
Section (i)	—	2	8	10	12	6
Section (ii)	—	—	11	11	11	3
Section (iii)	—	—	3	3	3	1
Sub-total	—	*2*	*22*	*24*	*26*	*10*
Total	*20*	*25*	*122*	*167*	*232*	*51*
C. Initiator's parish-section:						
Agnates	2	2	12	14	22	2
Non-agnatic cognates	7	8	69	84	106	13
Indirect affines	—	—	3	3	3	2
Sub-total	*9*	*10*	*84*	*101*	*131*	*17*
Initiator's parish – other sections:						
Section (i)	5	6	31	42	58	4
Section (ii)	—	—	4	4	4	2
Section (iii)	1	—	2	2	4	1
Section (iv)	—	—	2	2	2	1
Sub-total	*6*	*6*	*39*	*50*	*68*	*8*
Total	*15*	*16*	*123*	*151*	*199*	*25*
Grand total	*50*	*58*	*387*	*492*	*658*	*108*

each, and in section C, four deaths. Huli value sows, gilts and barrows differently, so I compute weighted values, giving the barrow unit value, the gilt two and a breeding sow three. This converts pig values into standard units.

For the 14 reparation payments, 108 donors contributed 492 pigs with a standard value of 658 units. The average value of the payments is 47 units and the average contribution per donor is 6 units. The greater proportion of donors, 78 per cent, are members of the initiator's section, and the value of their contributions is 85 per cent of the total.

The initiator sends word to the victim's brother or next-of-kin when he is ready to make the agreed payment. A time and place is set for the exchange, usually on a parish-territory of the victim. The victim's next-of-kin sends word to his bilateral relatives wherever they may be living. Word spreads quickly, for a distribution is an important social event. On the appointed day the dead man's relatives assemble. Their creditors too are present, ready to press their claims at the first opportunity. Many people with no material interest in the distribution come to watch.

The donors carry or lead their pigs to the meeting ground where they tether them in lines of fifteen. The victim's next-of-kin inspects each line, rejecting sick or malformed animals. Men of the initiator's section declaim the generousness of the payment, the excellence of the pigs and their own self-denial in giving their entire stock. In reply, the kin of the dead man deprecate the payment offered and bemoan their inconsolable loss.

With the speeches in progress, the potential recipients silently weigh the merits of their claims. Each mentally decides the share he should receive and which particular pig would suit him. The victim's next-of-kin then accepts the payment. Now the donors are free to leave, for they have no voice in the distribution. Sometimes the payment is distributed fully on the spot. At other times it is divided equally between the patri- and matrilateral kin. A father or brother then distributes the patrilateral share, while a mother's brother or maternal cousin takes charge of the matrilateral portion. Anyone who has been socially important to the victim expects to receive a share of the payment. The persons with the strongest claim are members of the elementary family and the mother's brother of the dead man, the men with whom he resided, people who killed pigs when he was ill or dying and contributors to any of his funerary payments.

A typical example of the distribution of reparations is that made at the death of Yulupe, a ten-year old boy killed by men of Twadia parish. Yulupe's father fought against Twadia and the initiator paid him reparation totalling 30 items. The payment was made following an epidemic pig disease, so cowrie shell necklaces were substituted for some pigs.

TABLE 25. RECIPIENTS OF REPARATIONS FOR YULUPE'S DEATH

Recipient	Item	Relationship to Yulupe
Patrilateral:		
1. Pogama	1 sow	Father
2. All participants in feast	1 gilt	—
3. Hidibi	2 barrows	Indirect affine*
4. Lawi	1 barrow	*FaMoBrSn*
5. Dagama	1 barrow	Distant class. FaMoBrSn**
6. Piowigia	1 barrow	*FaBr* *
7. Agilu	1 barrow	Distant class. FaBr**
8. Mindidi	1 cowrie neckpiece	*FaMoSsSn* *
9. Togure	1 cowrie neckpiece	*FaMoSsSn* *
10. Pagiabe	1 cowrie neckpiece	Distant class. FaSsSn*
11. Kili	1 cowrie neckpiece	Distant class. FaSsSn
12. Agoma	1 barrow and 1 steel axe	Close class. FaBrDaHu*
13. Mima	1 cowrie neckpiece	Fa of Agoma (12)*
Matrilateral:		
14. Hobe	1 sow, 1 barrow 1 cowrie neckpiece	Close class. MoFaBrSn*
15. Dindube	1 gilt	Close class. MoFaBrSc*
16. Botago	1 barrow	*MoFaMoBrSnSn* *
17. Hara	1 pearlshell	Distant class. MoBaFr*
18. Dugodia	1 cowrie neckpiece	*MoFaMoBrSnSn* **
19. Maria	1 cowrie neckpiece	*MoFaFaSsSnSn*
20. Kurunali	2 cowrie neckpieces	Distant class. MoFaBr
21. Yabe	1 barrow	Indirect affine*
22. Yegere	1 barrow	Indirect affine*
23. Yai	1 barrow	Unrelated friend of 1*
24. Porpo	1 barrow	Unrelated friend of 1
25. Mara	1 cowrie neckpiece	Indirect affine*
Total	30 items	

* Contributors to funerary payment.
** Contributors to propitiatory offering for Yulupe's illness. Italics indicate actual rather than classificatory relationship.

Pogama, the victim's father, distributed the patrilateral share, and Hobe distributed the matrilateral share. (Yulupe's mother and mother's brothers were all dead.) Of the 25 recipients, 15 had

COMPENSATION

TABLE 26. DISTRIBUTION OF REPARATIONS FOR THE DEATH OF TEABE'S WIFE

Recipients	Item	Relationship to Teabe

Part I:

1.	Teabe	3 sows	*Ego*
2.	Padilu	1 gilt	*MoMoBrSn* *
3.	Lawi	1 gilt	Close class. MoBrSn**
4.	Dugube	1 gilt and 2 barrows	Dead Wife's Fa
5.	Dagiabe	1 barrow	Distant class. MoBr**
6.	Lidoli	1 barrow	Indirect affine
7.	Lidoli's *WiMo*	1 barrow	Indirect affine***
8.	Tomiabe	1 barrow	Friend***
9.	Halimba	1 barrow	*FaBrSn****
10.	Igibe	1 barrow	*Br*
11.	Dabale	1 barrow	Close class. MoSsSn***
12.	Lengo	1 barrow	Close class. MoSsSn***
13.	Kuri	1 barrow	Close class. MoSsSn***
14.	Urulu	1 barrow	Distant class. FaBrSn
15.	Biyago	1 barrow	Ss
16.	Pulume	1 barrow	Ss
17.	Hewome	1 barrow	Ss***

Part II: Additional Pigs Added by Teabe:

18.	Ngibe	1 gilt	Close class. MoSsSn***
19.	Harinda	1 gilt	*FaMoSsSn****
20.	Dago	1 barrow	*FaSsSn****
21.	Lulu	1 barrow	*FaMoBrSn****
22.	Orabe	1 barrow	*FaMoBrSn****
23.	Nabili	1 barrow	Distant class. FaBrSn***
24.	Kara	1 barrow	Close class. FaSsSn***
25.	Dadabu	1 barrow	*FaFaMoSsSn* *
26.	Tili	1 barrow	*FaFaMoSsSn* *
27.	Kedalu	1 barrow	*FaFaMoSnSn* *
28.	Hiyera	1 barrow	*FaFaFaMoSsSnSn* *
29.	Harigeli	1 barrow	Close class. MoSsSn
30.	Lema	1 barrow	Close class. MoSsSn

Total   35 items

* Formerly donated pigs to reparations paid by Teabe.
** Contributed to Teabe's bride price for dead wife.
*** Contributed to funerary payments for dead wife.

contributed to at least one of Yulupe's funerary payments, that is, to the fees for the corpse-handlers, body-bearers, or to donors to the mortuary feast. Of the 10 contributors, 3 received shares specifically because they had donated pigs to the child's father (for propitiatory offerings) when Yulupe had been sick. The other 7 received shares because of their kinship with Pogama and Hobe.

Of the 12 patrilateral recipients, 9 are members of Yulupe's agnatic section, 1 is a member of another section of his agnatic parish, and the other 4 belong to his father's mother's (agnatic) parish-section. Of the matrilateral recipients, 10 belong to his mother's (agnatic) section, and 2 to other sections of her (agnatic) parish.

Teabe was not obliged to give a large portion of the reparations to his dead wife's relatives. He had previously received fifteen pigs in wergild from his wife's killer, and he had given all but two pigs to his affines. Nevertheless, when his dead wife's father appeared at the distribution, Teabe was shamed by his presence and gave him a gilt and two barrows. With the exception of his father-in-law, all of the people who received pigs were people who stood in some relationship with Teabe. Several men had formerly contributed to reparations paid by Teabe; a few had contributed to his bride price; some had contributed to the funerary payments for his dead wife.

Both of the above examples are atypical in one respect—the payment was distributed peacefully. Usually the large pigs are distributed in an orderly fashion, but as the number of pigs remaining grows smaller, arguments arise over who should have them. Men excluded from the allocation claim against the original initiator. Whether he can be intimidated depends on the status of the claimant and his ability to muster force to back his claim. An initiator in this position may prefer to give an extra pig, rather than precipitate another war for which he will again bear responsibility.

The obligation to pay reparations has a divisive effect on the group that fought together. In addition, the longer the payments are delayed, the greater the dissatisfaction among the victim's kin. Nevertheless, the obligation serves to unite men of the parish-section, at least until the payments are completed. Restrictions are placed on marriage and ritual while the obligation lasts, and the common endeavour to discharge a heavy obligation binds them together.

C. WERGILD[1]

The initiator with his parish-section is obliged to pay wergild to the enemy only in minor wars. The purpose of wergild is to deter retalia-

---

1. Kapauku also distinguish between reparation and wergild; they call reparation *uwata*, "a payment made by the man for whom the hostilities were conducted" (Huli war-initiator) "to the closest relative of a slain man who fought on . . . (his) side; and wergild, *me mege*". POSPISIL 1958:93.

COMPENSATION

tion before a fight develops into large-scale war. The enemy who accepts wergild cannot take vengeance—exacting vengeance and accepting wergild for the same death provokes supernatural punishment. The deities are angered by such duplicity and cause sickness or misfortune to those who attempt it. No wergild is payable in a full-scale war, for once the involvement has reached a certain magnitude, it becomes impossible for one man or one faction to control the war-party. The initiator often wishes to stop the fighting as the casualties mount, but he is seldom able to do so. Because of this, no wergild is paid once several casualties have occurred on both sides.

Huli also describe as 'wergild' a payment a man makes for killing his own kin during a fight. This payment should be made no matter what the magnitude of the fight, whether or not the slayer is the initiator, and whether or not the killing was accidental. This kin-wergild is a personal responsibility; a man cannot call on his section mates for assistance, though some may volunteer to help him. The size of the payment ranges from seven to fifteen pigs, which are distributed among the victim's bilateral kin in the same way as reparations.

In the payment of ordinary wergild, donors again assist the initiator. Table 27 shows the donors and their contributions to four wergild payments.

TABLE 27. CONTRIBUTIONS TO HULI WERGILD PAYMENTS

Donor	*Sows*	*Gilts*	*Barrows*	*All*	*Value*	*No. of Donors*
Initiator's parish-section:						
Agnates	7	5	19	31	50	5
Non-agnatic cognates	2	2	2	6	12	3
Direct affines	—	—	7	7	7	4
Indirect affines	—	2	1	3	5	3
Other	1	1	3	5	8	1
Sub-total	*10*	*10*	*32*	*52*	*82*	*16*
Initiator's parish – other sections:						
Section (i)	—	1	2	3	4	2
Section (ii)	—	1	7	8	9	5
Sub-total	*—*	*2*	*9*	*11*	*13*	*7*
Total	10	12	41	63	95	23

It is possible for the kin of a war victim to receive reparations from the initiator's parish-section, wergild from the enemy parish-section and personal wergild from the slayer. In fact, reparation payments are the most common. For the deaths of 119 war victims, the initiators' sections paid reparations for 82 deaths and promised payments for 15 others; in 9 instances no reparation could be claimed, for the victim was in fact the initiator. For the same deaths, the victim's kin received 25 wergild payments from the enemy initiator's section and 5 payments of personal wergild from the dead man's slayer. Reparations are not only paid more often than wergild, they are paid at a higher scale. Table 24 shows that reparations for 14 deaths totalled 658 standard units, an average of 47 units. By comparison, Table 27 shows that for 4 deaths, the average wergild is 24 standard units.

The bilateral kin of the victim are entitled to wergild, just as they are to reparation. In personal wergild, where the payment is relatively small, the span of kin who receive it is limited. People who fail to obtain a share from wergild press their claims again when reparations are paid.

D. Case Studies

So far I have described the general characteristics of the Huli indemnity system. The following two cases present the system in operation. They show the ramifications of apparently simple events. They show men reaching decisions and dealing with the problem of responsibility for losses and injury in war. They also indicate how groups mobilize in support of individuals and how some individuals evade their obligations to the groups of which they are ostensibly members.

Case 1. Residence and Responsibility

In 1953 Harikondo of Tunda-*Nenya* was killed while serving as an ally of Halongo-*Pelupe*. After the fight, Halongo men paid 15 pigs to Tunda-*Nenya* as the patrilateral half of reparations, but gave nothing to Kegeta-*Pogore* men, who were entitled to the matrilateral share.

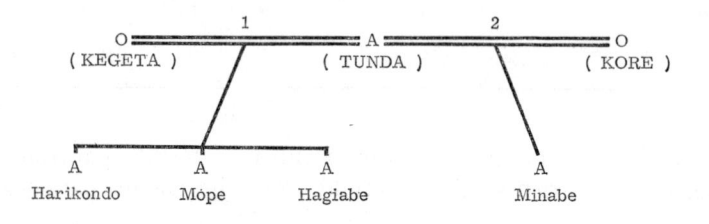

```
              1                    2
      O===========A===========O
   ( KEGETA )   ( TUNDA )   ( KORE )


      A        A        A              A
   Harikondo  Mope   Hagiabe         Minabe
```

Harikondo's brother, Mope, and his half-brother, Minabe, both of whom lived on Kegeta-*Pogore* territory, were angered by this omission and decided to seize some *Pelupe* pigs in order to force the defaulters to pay. Late one afternoon, Mope and Minabe went to Halongo territory to search for pigs but they were unsuccessful. On their way home, they crossed Pi-*Hata* territory, where they saw a large sow grubbing unattended in marsh ground. Minabe proposed that they steal this pig, but Mope, who was cognatically related to Pi-*Hata* men and had recently lived on their territory, rejected the suggestion. Although Minabe was annoyed by this refusal, he went off with Mope to Librua-territory, where both (as multilocal residents) lived for part of each year. That night Minabe again urged that they steal the sow. Again Mope opposed the theft, but at length suggested that Minabe steal it without him. Minabe set off quickly, accompanied by Angau of Librua, and killed the pig. Together they carried the carcase for about a mile to Kore-territory, where Minabe had close kinsmen.

The owner of the sow discovered his loss that same night and by chance met some men who had seen Minabe and Angau carrying the carcase. With several of his kinsmen the owner set out for Kore-territory, and the pig was still cooking when the party arrived.

Minabe and Angau, however, heard them approach, and they fled to Librua-territory, which was about five miles away. When the Pi-*Hata* party threatened the Kore men, the latter disclaimed responsibility and blamed Minabe and Angau for the theft. The Pi-*Hata* men, not knowing where the culprits had fled, went to Kegeta-*Pogore*-territory and claimed theft compensation of eight pigs from the men with whom Minabe had recently been living. The Kegeta-*Pogore* men also denied responsibility for the theft, and after a heated argument a fight broke out between the two groups. The fight lasted for four days, and one man, Kaube of Pi-*Hata* was killed. Although Kaube had fought with, and was a member of Pi-*Hata*, he was an agnate of Kegeta-*Pogore*. Consequently, when he died, both sides agreed to a truce and jointly mourned his loss. Because of Kaube's dual affiliation, neither parish-section compensated the other for his death; but both compensated Agona-*Eyagu*, his mother's (agnatic) parish-section, which in turn distributed the payments to other kinsmen of Kaube. Pi-*Hata* made reparation of forty-five pigs. Kegeta-*Pogore* men, without donations from Mope or Minabe, paid a wergild of fifteen pigs.

TABLE 28. CONTRIBUTIONS TO KAUBE'S WERGILD

Donor	Contribution	Donor's relationship to agnatic ancestors of Kegeta-Pogore
Wagi	1 sow	Fa
Harabe	1 sow	Mo
Pepe	1 gilt	MoMo
Ilubwa	1 barrow	FaMo
Mindidi	1 barrow	FaFaMo
Telabe	1 barrow	FaFaMo
Tege	1 barrow	Mo
Uri	1 barrow	Fa
Kane	1 barrow	Fa
Wabubu	1 barrow	FaFaFaMoMo
Marabe	1 barrow	FaFaMo
Pagidia	1 barrow	FaFaMoMo
Hagiabe	1 barrow	FaFaFaMo
Twali	1 barrow	FaFaFaMo
Padilia	1 barrow	FaFaFaMo
Total	*15 pigs*	

During the fight between *Hata* and *Pogore*, Arago, an ally of Kegeta-*Pogore*, was wounded in the back. He recovered, but the arrow-point could not be removed from his chest. Three years later the wound became infected around the impacted arrow-tip and Arago suffered great pain. After consulting a diviner, he dedicated and killed his pigs one by one as propitiatory offerings to the deities, hoping to gain relief. When he had no more pigs, he claimed wound-compensation from the Kegeta-*Pogore* men. They refused to pay, giving as an excuse their payment of wergild for killing Kaube in a fight which they did not initiate. They told Arago to claim instead from Minabe and Mope.

After the theft of the original pig, neither Mope nor Minabe had returned to Kegeta-territory, but had settled on Librua-territory. When faced with Arago's claim, they fell out with one another. Mope asserted that he had not sanctioned the original theft and, therefore, the responsibility was Minabe's; Minabe in turn said that Mope had condoned the act, and he refused to pay compensation unless Mope contributed half. This was still the situation in 1957.

In 1958, Mope and Minabe agreed to pay jointly, but by 1959 they had not done so. Each time Arago renewed his demand, they tried to evade the issue. On one occasion, Minabe contended that Halongo-*Pelupe* men were really responsible for Arago's injury; it was their failure to pay reparation originally to Kegeta that had led him to steal a pig in the first place. Most men who have heard Minabe's argument regard it as specious, for the stolen pig did not belong to Halongo.

The issue remained unsettled late in 1959, but Arago had lost patience. Friends said that he had become short-tempered and secretive, and that he had begun to plant new gardens in a distant parish-territory. On several occasions Arago was seen walking alone at night near Librua-territory. People say that vengeance "weighs on his heart" and he may soon try to murder Minabe and Mope for refusing to meet their obligation.

This case-history illustrates the way a man can renounce membership in a parish-section in order to avoid the consequences of his own misdeeds. In this situation, although the other men of the offender's section were in no way culpable, the aggrieved man called them to account. Consequently, Mope and Minabe are no longer welcome in Kegeta-*Pogore*-territory, but no member of *Pogore* is likely to take vengeance against them. Indeed, if they made restitution, *Pogore* men would probably reinstate them as members of the section.

Case 2. The Consequences of a Seduction

The seduction of the girl Wandume (Kore-*Kimabe*) by Ligia (Tugure-*Kili*), in 1953, initiated a chain of events which had repercussions for several years. At the time Ligia was engaged to Wandume and she was living with his first wife, a Kore-*Tare* woman who was also her classificatory sister. One day Ligia invited Wandume to meet him in the forest and, with her consent, they had intercourse. Later Wandume told Ligia's wife what had happened, and then left to visit her brother in Kore-territory. She also told him of her seduction and asked him to arrange her wedding to Ligia.

Her brother visited Ligia on the following day and proposed the match, but Ligia refused, insisting that he had no pigs for the bride price. An argument developed, which flared into a fight, and men of Kore-*Kimabe* attacked Tugure-*Kili*. The skirmish lasted for an afternoon and only one man was killed—Obi of Kore-*Ibi*, an ally of Kore-*Kimabe*. Obi's father, Mindidi, intervened and called for a truce to bury him. Mindidi feared that, if he did not propose the truce and a major war developed, he might be considered the initiator.

Mongobe of Tugure-*Ingu*, an ally of Tugure-*Kili*, also pressed for settlement out of sympathy for Mindidi, to whom he was distantly related. Soon afterwards, Kore-*Kimabe* men paid Mindidi 60 pigs as reparation for his son's death, and as the fight was a small one, Tugure-*Kili* gave him 30 pigs in wergild. Mindidi distributed most of the reparations to Obi's paternal and maternal kin, except those of Kore-*Ibi*. He kept several pigs from the wergild himself and gave the rest to other members of *Ibi* section.

Obi's mother, a Waga woman, had died long before, and Mindidi sent his second son, Dabe, to the Waga with her share of Obi's reparations. On arrival, however, Dabe was slain in a fight. Twice bereaved, Mindidi purchased *Toro* sorcery to avenge the death of his second son.

Several months after Mindidi had purchased the sorcery, Mongobe's young son took sick and died suddenly. No *post-mortem* was performed, but Mongobe assuming his son's death was the result of sorcery, called in a diviner. Guided by a bespelled *waru* stick, the sorcerer came to the place where Obi had died. The diviner himself did not voice an opinion, but Mongobe naturally assumed that Mindidi's sorcery had killed his son. Next day Mongobe accused Mindidi, but he denied directing sorcery at Tugure-territory. In the argument that followed, Mindidi's sister's son swore a ritual oath asserting his uncle's innocence. Shortly afterwards, an agnate of Kore-*Ibi* died, a man who had never lived on *Ibi* territory or maintained social relationships with other *Ibi* men. Mongobe insisted that the fact that the dead man was an *Ibi* by descent was sufficient proof of Mindidi's guilt. Mindidi rejected the accusation. Gaining no satisfaction from Mindidi, Mongobe then demanded compensation from Ligia as the original war-initiator. Ligia, however, denied culpability for the death of Mongobe's son, which he contended was unconnected with the fight; Ligia argued that Mindidi had employed sorcery and was therefore responsible.

Angered by this double rebuttal, Mongobe bought *Toro* sorcery to use against Mindidi. When the preparations were complete, he gave a *Mali* dance to announce his purchase. While the dance was in progress Mindidi's third son, a youth of 14 years, happened to pass by the dance-ground. Angered by the sight of the boy, and thinking of his own son, Mongobe seized a bow and shot him dead. This killing provoked a fight between Tugure-*Ingu* and Kore-*Ibi* which mobilised about 200 men in each war-party and lasted for four days. Two men, both on the *Ibi* side, were killed and their patrilateral kinsmen intervened to bury them. A truce called for the funeral ended hostilities. *Ibi* section later paid reparations of 45 pigs for each victim and *Ingu* paid wergild of 15 pigs apiece. Both payments were received by the paternal and maternal kin of the victims.

Until 1959 no reparations had been paid to Mindidi for the death of his third son, and Mongobe refused to pay wergild unless Mindidi first paid him compensation for the death of Mongobe's son. Although *Ingu* men had paid wergild for the deaths of Mugaga and Kimeli, the two victims, Mongobe still considered that Ligia, the original initiator, should be held responsible. In any case, *Ingu* men had paid Kimeli's wergild only because his agnatic section threatened to attack them if they withheld it.

Although Mongobe regards Mindidi as responsible for his (Mongobe's) son's death, he nevertheless feels sorry for him—all three of Mindidi's sons have been killed, and he has received little help in paying the reparations for allies wounded in the Ibi-*Ingu* clash. Four *Ibi* allies sustained serious arrow wounds in this fight and Mindidi has personally paid two of them wound-reparation totalling 45 pigs. He has not yet indemnified the other two men.

After Mindidi had paid the reparations for Mugaga, trouble flared up for him from another source. Men of Twadia, dissatisfied with their share of the payment for Mugaga, demanded more pigs from Mindidi. Mindidi refused, and the men of Twadia attacked Kore-*Ibi*, thus setting off another war.

In 1959, Mindidi was pressed for wound-reparation by the other two men who had fought as his allies against Tugure-*Ingu*. Mindidi acknowledged their claims but argued that, as he had lost his three sons and had already paid 150 pigs in reparations, Kore-*Kimabe* (who had originally attacked Tugure-*Kili* as a result of Ligia's seduction of Wandume) ought to assume responsibility for the two wound claims. The *Kimabe* men refused to do so. They insisted that two separate issues were involved, and that Mindidi was responsible because he had employed sorcery to kill Mongobe's son.

Members of other sections of Kore parish tried to mediate in the dispute, and they appealed to the *Kimabe* men to help Mindidi as they were all Kore men. *Kimabe* rejoined that a *Kimabe* agnate had wed an *Ibi* agnate and, therefore, the parish tie between the two sections was broken. When I left Tari this issue was still unsettled. Mindidi, an old man bereft of his sons, yet proud of the obligations he has discharged with little help, has returned to *Ibi*-territory, far from the protection of the government officers. Men not personally involved in the dispute applaud Mindidi's behaviour and condemn the *Kimabe* failure to pay the small claims for wound-damages. Outsiders who hazard an opinion say that, whether or not *Kimabe* men are jurally responsible, they should help Mindidi, for Mindidi once fought as their ally.

Mongobe, on the other hand, had some success in obtaining reparations for his son's death from Ligia. Ligia's section, Tugure-*Kili*, paid him 15 pigs. However, it is unlikely that Mongobe will succeed in recovering from them any of the wergild that he paid for the deaths of Mugaga and Kimeli. *Kili* men regard their payment to Mongobe as a quit-claim, and their willingness to pay was stimulated by their desire to restore friendly relations with *Ingu* before claiming against the latter on a different issue.

The complexity of this sequence of events is typical of most cases where jural responsibility is at issue. The people have no final means of adjudication, no tests more certain than ritual oaths to establish responsibility. This history has illustrated the independence of sections of the same parish; it shows too, that men do not always agree whether a given genealogical unit comprises one parish or has become two by segmentation.

E. Descent and Indemnity

In Chapter IV, I suggested that in Huli society recognition of agnatic status within a cognatic system is mainly a structuring and classifying device. I argued that the critical rights and obligations are shared equally by agnates and non-agnatic cognates. It is true that evidence of comparative land-holding does not support this hypothesis, but I argued that where a surplus of arable land exists, rights in land are not crucial indices of section membership. Data presented in this chapter provide a further test of the significance of agnatic status. The figures presented in Tables 26 and 27 are summarized in the following Table.

TABLE 29. ANALYSIS OF CONTRIBUTIONS TO WERGILD AND REPARATIONS

Status	No. of contributors	Value of contribution	Mean contribution
Initiator's parish-section:			
Agnates	30	239	7.96
Non-agnatic cognates	41	350	8.53
Direct affines	11	22	2.00
Indirect affines	10	23	2.30
Friends	8	16	2.00
All	100	650	6.50
Other contributors	31	103	3.32
Total	*131*	*753*	*5.75*

As expected, the values of contributions by members of the initiator's section are greater than those of other contributors (chi squared = 8.22, df = 1, p > .01), and the values of cognatic section members are greater than those of affinal section members and 'friends' (chi squared = 31.6, df = 1, p > .01). The analysis shows most importantly that agnatic section members, in proportion to their numbers, contribute no more to indemnities than do non-agnatic cognates. The difference in contributions is not statistically significant (chi squared = .096, df = 1, p > .05). In other words, cognatic section members contribute to group indemnities without regard to their descent status. This result upholds the view that the parish is essentially a cognatic unit in which agnates do not have special status.

F. SUMMARY AND DISCUSSION

The Huli system of compensation is based on the principle that a man is jurally responsible for the consequences of his actions. When he initiates a war, a man becomes liable for reparations to anyone injured while fighting on his behalf, and to anyone who by mishap is killed by the enemy. In addition, the initiator is liable for wergild in small scale wars, and when he kills a kinsman fighting on the opposing side. Table 30 summarises the more important relationships between the initiator, his parish-section and those to whom reparations or wergild are due.

TABLE 30. SUMMARY OF MAIN COMPENSATION RELATIONSHIPS

Offence	Relation of donor to recipient
Reparation:	
Death of section member inflicted by enemy*	Initiator's section: Victim's bilateral kin except donors
Death of ally, inflicted by enemy	Initiator's section: Victim's bilateral kin
Section member wounded by enemy	Initiator: Victim
Death of neutral by mishap, inflicted by enemy	Initiator's section: Victim's bilateral kin
Wergild:	
Killing an enemy	Enemy-initiator's section: Victim's bilateral kin
Killing a kinsman fighting on enemy side	Killer: Victim's bilateral kin, except killer's section

* In this instance intra-section reparations are also paid.

The parish-section relies heavily on allies both from within and from outside the parish. This chapter shows that about 21 per cent of war fatalities occur within the initiator's parish-section, 50 per cent occur within the initiator's parish, while the remaining 50 per cent are allies who are not members of the initiator's parish. Warfare unites men not only at the parish-section level, but to some extent at the parish level, and beyond it. Although war creates no alliance among groups as such, it does bind individuals belonging to many parish-sections in well-defined jural relationships. These relationships are not necessarily enduring; any delay in paying reparations to allies who have suffered loss or injury tends to create strain among the men who have fought as one war-party. Prolonged delay increases the strain and often precipitates open conflict amongst allies. Furthermore, the allocation of reparations and wergild in itself often produces tension among the recipients. The distribution may turn the victim's paternal and maternal kin against one another, or a dissatisfied recipient may press the donors for more pigs, thereby creating new hostility. The interplay of vengeance and compensation mobilizes new but temporary combinations of allies and enemies. Because of this, Huli society does not produce enduring corporate groups larger than the parish-section.

CHAPTER VIII

COGNATIC SOCIETY

The Huli population is one of the largest cultural groupings in the New Guinea highlands, and Huli territory is one of the most extensive. Myths, legends and genealogies indicate that the people believe that their ancestors settled the Tari basin some twenty generations ago. They also believe that their social organisation—based on membership of cognatic parishes—has always been the same, and that their main rituals originated in the legendary past. It is uncertain just how long the Huli have inhabited the Tari basin, but the available evidence suggests that it has been for at least a few centuries. Huli social structure must not be considered as derivative or transitory, but as a well-developed, coherent system in its own right.

There is little evidence to indicate that environmental factors have determined the form of Huli society.[1] Nevertheless, the two are related, and it is clear that in some ways cognatic organisation is well suited to the environment at Tari. I give two illustrations of this point.

Arable land at Tari is both plentiful and productive. Gardens are mostly situated on level land, and tilling the soil is comparatively easy. Not only are gardens productive, but pigs flourished until the anthrax epidemics of the 1940's.[2] Before the epidemics, large herds were common and people were better able to meet their social obligations. Despite these favourable conditions, crops are damaged from

1. A contrasting instance has been reported from northern Dutch New Guinea. J. POUWER, reviewing a study by VAN DER LEEDEN of two small communities (68 and 71 members) in the Sarmi area, suggests that an ambilineal descent system is particularly well suited "to life in harsh circumstances or even in a marginal situation". 1960:112. For a review of Dutch research on this relationship see Bureau of Native Affairs, 1958.
2. MEGGITT 1956:92.

time to time by too little or too much rain. Huli fear drought in particular; the basin provides little natural water storage and they depend on regular rainfall for their water supply. Rainfall variations often affect only a limited area, and Huli try to counteract this by planting gardens in widely scattered territories. Cognatic descent facilitates this by providing a man with land rights in many places.

The second illustration concerns the relation of the terrain to warfare. In the open country at Tari, defensive warfare is difficult. There is little natural protection from ambush or attack, and men try to safeguard their settlements by trenching the borders of parish-territory. They dig ditches fifteen feet deep and plant thick groves of cane grass as a further obstacle. However, these measures are not particularly effective—at best they delay an attack, at worst they permit the enemy to approach unseen. Huli meet this topographical defect by residing multilocally. This ensures them asylum if one of their territories is threatened. The constant threat of warfare provides a strong incentive for maintaining widespread cognatic ties.

The susceptibility of Huli to the effects of rainfall variation and their vulnerability to attack do not, of course, explain why Huli society has developed along cognatic lines. Perhaps the question is unanswerable, or perhaps our current knowledge is inadequate. At present, all that can be said is that the environment at Tari is appropriate for the development of a cognatic system. Huli have not found it necessary to control and allocate resources by rigidly applying unilineal descent or other restrictive principles.

It is of interest to compare Huli society with Central Enga,[1] six days walk to the north and east.

	Central Enga	*Huli*
Population	60,000	30-40,000
Area	500 sq. miles	2,000 sq. miles
Overall density	120 per sq. mile	20 per sq. mile
Maximum density	220 per sq. mile	70 per sq. mile
Average elevation	7,000 feet	5,300 feet
Annual sweet potato yield	4.4 tons/acre	10 tons/acre
Group structure	localised agnatic lineages	cognatic parishes
Proportion of male agnates[2] in the parish	90 per cent	20 per cent

1. MEGGITT 1958:256.
2. MEGGITT uses 'putative' agnate in his account, "for it is clear . . . in each generation a number of attached members of a clan-parish, generally sons' children of a female agnate, automatically become 'agnatic' members of the clan". 1958:264. Thus, Huli and Enga define 'agnate' quite differently, and strictly speaking, a comparison of agnates in the descent systems cannot be made.

While Enga culture is similar to Huli in general orientation, Enga social organisation differs markedly. Agnatic descent and patrilocality are the chief principles of Enga group structure and they apply particularly in the control of arable land. In view of these facts, M. J. Meggitt has suggested the following hypothesis: "Where the members of a homogeneous society of agriculturalists distinguish in any consistent fashion between agnates and other relatives, the degree to which social groups are structured in terms of agnatic descent and patrilocality varies with the pressure on agrarian resources."[1]

My observations support this hypothesis in a negative way; land is not short, agnatic recruitment is not stressed and parishes are not organized into an elaborate segmentary system. Yet it is easy to see how, if the Huli population increased rapidly, their cognatic system could develop into one of agnatic lineages. The basis is already there —agnates control more land than other cognates, and with increasing scarcity of land they are more likely to defend their claims than to relinquish them. Certain factors in the contact situation may well accelerate this process. The population will probably grow rapidly as a result of medical care, infant welfare clinics and an improvement in the diet. At the same time, one of the chief motives for multilocal residence—the threat of warfare—will no longer operate, and the population may become more sedentary. The introduction of permanent cash crops could lead to a sharper definition of land rights. All of these factors may in the next two decades permit us to observe at Tari the transformation of a cognatic society to a unilineal one.

Big men, in their behaviour, demonstrate to the fullest the characteristic features of their society. The position of big men in Huli society differs considerably from that of big men in other highland societies.[2] In the unilineal societies with discrete political groups, the power of big men stems from their leadership and influence within a lineage, clan or phratry. In Huli society, the effective political group is a relatively small unit and it acts only sporadically as a corporate group. The big man establishes his position by participating as an individual in the affairs of not one but many parish groups. Because of his many parish ties and far-flung interests, he is often concerned in both sides of a dispute, and he can be instrumental in calling for peace, in negotiating compromise and in arranging indemnities. He takes part in social transactions over a very wide area. He contributes generously and often to indemnity and other payments, and by doing so he establishes claims against some groups to which he is not genealogically related.

1. 1959:277.
2. See READ 1959.

The process of becoming a big man may be viewed in three phases. The first covers the period from late adolescence to early manhood—just before marriage. Most young men were eager to take part in war—they enjoyed fighting for its own sake and were often not personally concerned with the issues that led to the fight. During this period, young men restrict their interests to one, or sometimes two parish-sections. The older men of the section make most of the important decisions, such as whether to fight a certain enemy, and when to make payments of reparation or wergild. The young man has limited influence in this decision-making, but he can be relied on to carry out decisions. In this first stage of his career, he is a partisan of only one or two groups, and he rarely acts independently or on his own initiative.

The second phase extends from the time he marries until middle age, the upper limit varying with the ambition of the individual. This phase is characterized by the expansion of a man's interests and the development of individual initiative. During this period he resides multilocally and he participates actively in the affairs of several parish-sections. When he is involved in conflicting claims, he may now choose one as the more important, or he may withdraw to another territory until the crisis passes. Many men never achieve status or prestige higher than this; as they grow older, the span of their social attachments diminishes, or at best remains the same.

Men who reach the third stage maintain still wider affiliations. They must be wealthy to meet their increased obligations, and for a good supply of pigs they need large gardens, and to maintain these they become polygynists. The most powerful men exert a regional influence, taking part in so many social activities that their name is well known over a wide area. Teabe, for example, was a member of six different parishes at one time and he was influential in the affairs of five others. He could trace genealogical relationships step by step to thirty-two parish groups, and during his life he had lived with or at least visited kin in twenty-four of these groups. The true big man behaves less often as a partisan of one particular group and more often as an arbiter among several. Nowadays he is active in settling indemnity disputes.

The coming of the Administration has not greatly altered the indigenous authority structure, but it has allowed some men to achieve recognition and power by non-traditional means. This point was made clear to me by the following incident.

Tagube was one of several boys who went to Wabag with a patrol of J. Taylor in 1939. There, he learned Pidgin-English, returning to Tari ten years later and becoming an Administration interpreter in 1953. Few Huli speak Pidgin (or Police Motu) and Tagube discovered that he could influence the decision of the court by distorting his translation of the evidence. At first, he helped only his kinsmen and friends, but later began to accept and demand bribes from other people. His duplicity was detected from time to time, but no more reliable interpreter was available to replace him. In the course of two years he acquired ten wives, a feat matched by few men in the past. His marriages increased the number of his social relationships and his status in native society soared. Huli became conscious of Tagube's dishonesty, and they complained bitterly among themselves, but lacked courage to approach the government officials.

Tagube lost his job after four years in government employ. He was discovered telling a flagrant lie, was fired and barely escaped criminal proceedings. Huli did not applaud his dismissal; the main reaction was one of sympathy. Even men who had lost court cases because of Tagube's dishonesty were sorry for him. As an official he had achieved the power and recognition of a bigman. At the height of his administrative career he no longer solicited bribes—people simply gave him a pig when the judgment was in their favour. Once he was accepted as a big man, his behaviour as an interpreter was regarded as an aspect of this status. As such, it was not condemned. Had Tagube been fired earlier in his career, his dismissal might have been more popular. Loss of official status came too late to check his social rise. He was not sorry to go—leaving the Administration gave him more freedom to conduct his own affairs. Today, wearing native dress and eating traditional food, Tagube still holds a powerful position in Huli society. He achieved his status by non-traditional means, but having done so, he behaves in the traditional manner of the successful man; he resides multilocally, his wives are spread among several parish-territories, he maintains many and widespread cognatic relationships and he is frequently called on to mediate in disputes.

Residential mobility is also characteristic of other societies in the western and southern highlands. But these societies—the Ipili,[1] the Waga,[2] and the Mendi[3] have fundamentally patrilineal institutions. D'Arcy Ryan has dealt with the problem of analysing the "modified or flexible patrilineal system" in which a high proportion of parish members are non-agnates.[4] He rightly points out the critical importance of differentiating the roles of patrikin and matrikin, especially in death payments. M. J. Meggitt makes a similar observation for the Waga[5] and Ipili.[6] He cites the critical case in an Ipili example:

1. MEGGITT 1957:38-39.
2. MEGGITT 1956:93-96.
3. RYAN 1959:280-281.
4. 1959:286.
5. 1956:105.
6. 1957:44.

when an agnatic parish resident dies, his patrikin make a substantial payment to his maternal agnates. If the dead man lived with his affines, his mother's mother's or father's father's clan, they act as patrikin and pay the maternal agnates. But if the man lived with his maternal kin, they give the mourning feast and no payment is necessary.

The distribution of death payments enables a clear distinction to be made between cognatic and 'flexible' agnatic societies. Huli have no death payments identical with those of the Ipili, Waga or Mendi, but their distribution of reparations and wergild provides a test. If a man dies fighting for his agnatic parish-section, the initiator pays half-scale reparation to his maternal relatives and a smaller payment to patrilateral kinsmen of his father's mother's (agnatic) section. Similarly, if a man dies while fighting for his mother's (agnatic) section, the initiator pays half-scale reparation to his patrilateral kin and a smaller payment to his mother's mother's (agnatic) section. The crucial point is that Huli view a man as being related in the same way to both matri- and patrikin. It is the presence of patrilineal institutions, not the norms of parish recruitment, that are diacritical for agnatic society.

Cognatic systems have been documented in two other Melanesian societies, the To'ambaita of northern Malaita[1] and the people of Möwehafen in southwestern New Britain.[2] Fragmentary evidence recently reviewed by H. Ian Hogbin and Camilla Wedgwood[3] suggests that cognatic societies are also present in Sio Island off the coast of New Britain,[4] among the Koiari of the Central District of Papua[5] and in the Eddystone Islands in the British Solomons.[6]

In To'ambaita society men reckon parish genealogies of up to twenty-six generations. Descent is traced through both males and females and every man has potential rights in the parish groups wherever he has an ancestor buried. Periodically, ancestor-rites attract non-resident parish members and those who fail to attend "signify by their absence that they have relinquished their right to live in the parish-territory and to be regarded as potential members of the parish."[7] In addition, To'ambaita distinguish terminologically between agnates and non-agnatic cognates and they grade the latter as children of female agnates and grandchildren of female

1. HOGBIN 1939.
2. TODD 1935a and b; 1936.
3. 1953:261-263.
4. GROVES 1935.
5. WILLIAMS 1921.
6. RIVERS 1924:13 and 42.
7. HOGBIN and WEDGWOOD 1953:262.

agnates. This classification is identical in principle with that of the Huli and it may well serve the same function—to structure internal relationships among parish members related by complex genealogical ties. In these respects, To'ambaita and Huli societies are similar.

To'ambaita differ from Huli in that their parishes apparently include a high proportion of agnates, and residential mobility is less common. Despite an emphasis on personal freedom "most men prefer to go on living where they have been reared, and not more than one in ten changes over to a new place . . . change of residence occurs as a rule only where there is ill-feeling as the result of a quarrel, or if luck has been consistently bad, or if a man's immediate paternal kinsmen have died and he wishes perhaps to join forces with his maternal relatives."[1] Unfortunately, Hogbin's account does not provide quantitative data about the range of recognised descent ties and the frequency with which they are employed. While To'ambaita may well recognise as many descent ties as Huli, their residential stability suggests that they make far less use of them.

A. J. Todd has recorded cognatic parishes called *endit* in southwestern New Britain. These are of shallow genealogical depth and a person belongs to "his father's, his mother's, those of their parents and so on."[2] The people are residentially mobile and one explicit reason for this is their desire to maintain land rights in several places. Another is to escape frequent intra-parish quarrels arising out of sorcery.[3] Todd's statements about land availability are difficult to interpret. He mentions that the population was low (in 1935) as a result of a smallpox epidemic thirty years earlier,[4] and he also reports that land disputes were frequent.[5] We cannot be sure, therefore, whether or not land was actually scarce.

The people of Möwehafen differ from Huli in important respects. Cross-cousin marriage is permitted and exogamous rules are less restrictive. This tends to limit the spread of a person's descent ties. In addition, there is some development of hereditary rank.

Unfortunately, sufficient data are not available for a full comparison of To'ambaita, Möwehafen and Huli societies, but the line such a study should take is clear. We need to know in To'ambaita and Möwehafen what range of affiliative choice is available to the individual, and how often and on what basis choices are made. It is also important to discover the extent of multiple group membership and the incidence of multilocal residence. Information of this sort from other

1. Hogbin 1939:27.
2. 1935b:457.
3. 1935a:91.
4. 1935a:91.
5. 1936:420.

cognatic societies as well may enable a typology to be constructed. Tentatively, two important variables can be isolated. A cognatic system may provide a wide or relatively narrow range of affiliative possibilities for the individual. Huli and To'ambaita societies are examples of the former, while Möwehafen probably exemplifies the latter. Societies may also differ in the extent to which the possible affiliative ties are actually exploited. Huli and Möwehafen appear to make use of a large proportion of potential ties while To'ambaita employ a comparatively small proportion. Another form cognatic society could take is to provide a narrow affiliative range of which only a small proportion is utilised. The relatively stable ramages of Polynesia may belong to this class.

Proportion of affiliative possibilities exploited	*Range of affiliative possibilities*	
	Wide	Narrow
High	Huli	Möwehafen
Low	To'ambaita	Polynesian systems?

Comparative analyses of cognatic societies and the construction of an adequate typology must await the publication of full accounts from more societies. Many anthropologists have recently begun to supply such accounts and progress has been made towards a standard terminology, a general classification and a preliminary theoretical analysis.

It is now nearly a generation since Paul Kirchoff called attention to the existence and importance of descent groups that are non-unilinear in structure.[1] In 1953 H. Ian Hogbin and Camilla Wedgwood published a survey and a new classification of the forms of local grouping in Melanesia. In 1955 Ward H. Goodenough contributed to our understanding of non-unilinear groups while studying a problem in Malayo-Polynesian social organisation. He shows how non-unilinear descent groups function as land-holding units in the Gilbert Islands, among the Ifugao and in several Polynesian societies. In 1956 Raymond Firth summarized the structural characteristics of Polynesian descent groups. In 1958 J. D. Freeman's analysis of Iban agriculture appeared, adding substantially to knowledge of bilateral

---

1. His paper, called "The Principles of Clanship in Human Society", circulated among anthropologists during the 1940's, but was not published until 1955. It has recently been reprinted in M. FRIED's *Readings in Anthropology*.

society. In 1959 William Davenport re-analysed the concept of non-unilinear descent and showed that knowledge of non-unilinear systems helps us to understand unilinear systems.

In the last ten years, the number of descriptive terms for non-unilinear systems has increased substantially. Our present armory of concepts includes "restricted and unrestricted descent groups" (Goodenough),[1] "ramage" (Firth),[2] "sept" (Davenport after Boaz),[3] "ambilineage" (Leach),[4] "ambilateral lineages" (White),[5] "non-carpellary parish" (Hogbin and Wedgwood)[6] and "kindred group" (Fortes).[7]

In 1960 George P. Murdock constructed a typology for non-unilinear systems and suggested a standard terminology. As a general term contrasting with 'unilineal' he proposed that 'cognatic' should be applied "to any grouping of kinsmen organised by genealogical ties without particular emphasis on either patrilineal or matrilineal connections."[8] He delineated three kinds of cognatic system by applying nine structural criteria to sample societies in the Human Relations Area Files. He calls the three systems bilateral, quasi-unilineal and ambilineal, and Huli society clearly falls into the latter. Whether or not Murdock's terminology becomes generally accepted, I believe the discriminations he makes are significant. Even more important is his insistence that classification should be based on statistical norms rather than on jural rules, a view he shares with E. R. Leach. Leach elaborated the view in his study of Pul Eliya village in Ceylon:

"It is my thesis that jural rules and statistical norms should be treated as separate frames of reference, but that the former should always be considered secondary to the latter."[9]

I have endeavoured to discover the structure of Huli society by studying the behaviour of people both as group members and as individuals. This approach was necessary, for Huli society permits wide affiliative choice and residential mobility. It was essential to make a quantitative study to test the association between such variables as age and marital status in relation to residence, or descent and residence in relation to land-holding. The significance of the study lies not in the general conclusion that Huli society is essentially

1. 1955:72-73.
2. 1957:6.
3. 1959:563-564.
4. 1950-61-62.
5. 1959:176-177.   (The MS for this volume was apparently completed in 1950.)
6. 1958:261-262.
7. 1959:213-214.
8. 1960:2.
9. 1961:9.

cognatic, but in the relationships that were discovered to exist among the variables. It is not possible to predict the behaviour of an individual in Huli society, but given a certain fact about a person's status, such as his mode of affiliation to a group, it is possible to assess the likelihood that he will be a land-holder (or a non-land-holder), a unilocal (or multilocal) resident or that he will belong in any of the other categories that have been the subject of analysis. It is in the cumulation of such statements of probability that the structure of the society consists.

APPENDIX I

ACREAGE OF TUNDA GARDENS HELD BY INDIVIDUALS
IN DIVIDED OWNERSHIP, 1960

Provisional title-holder	\multicolumn{6}{c}{Acreage held by residual title-holder}
	Fa	Mo	FaMo	MoMo	Other cognate	Total
Same parish-section:						
Fa	.9	.2				1.1
Mo	.2			.2		.4
FaMo	.3					.3
MoMo					.4	.4
Other cognate				1.9		1.9
Direct affine	4.7				.7	5.4
Indirect affine	1.3		.2		.3	1.8
Total	*7.4*	*.2*	*.2*	*2.1*	*1.4*	*11.3*
Other parish-sections:						
Fa	1.1				.7	1.8
Mo	1.3		.2		.6	2.1
FaMo						
MoMo	1.4		.1			1.5
Other cognate	1.3	.2	.1	.2	.2	2.0
Direct affine	.3		.1		.5	.9
Indirect affine			1.2		.5	1.7
Total	*5.4*	*.2*	*1.7*	*.2*	*2.5*	*10.0*
Unrelated friends	.7		.5		.4	1.6
Grand total	*13.5*	*.4*	*2.4*	*2.3*	*4.3*	*22.9*

APPENDIX II

Acreage Held in Full and Residual Titles by Members of Tunda Parish, 1960

Membership category	Men Number	Per cent	Acreage Number	Per cent	Mean acres per man
Resident					
Unilocal:					
Agnates	8	10.1	22.7	24.3	2.84
Non-agnatic cognates:*					
Mo	1		2		
MoMo	1		.3		
MoFaMo	1		1.0		
FaFaFaMo	1		1.0		
MoMoFaMo	1		.4		
MoFaFaMo	1		.5		
FaFaFaFaMo	1		.4		
All	7	8.9	5.6	6	.80
Non-cognates	2	2.5	.4	.4	.20
All unilocal	17	21.5	28.7	30.7	1.69
Multilocal:					
Agnates	12	15.2	18	19.3	1.50
Non-agnatic cognates:					
FaMo	3		2.1		
MoMo	4		5.6		
FaFaMo	2		4.0		
FaMoMo	1		1.0		
MoFaMo	3		2.0		
MoMoMo	1		.6		
FaFaFaMo	6		8.3		
FaFaMoMo	1		.7		
FaMoFaMo	1		1.0		

APPENDIX II. *Continued*

FaMoMoMo	1		1.3		
MoMoFaMo	1		2.9		
All	24	30.4	29.5	31.5	1.23
Non-cognates	2	2.5	.4	.4	.20
All Multilocal	38	48.1	47.9	51.2	1.23
Total residents	55	69.5	76.6	82.1	1.39

Non-resident

Agnates	3	3.8	4	4.3	1.43
Non-agnatic cognates:					
Mo	1		1.5		
FaMo	6		3.2		
MoMo	4		1.0		
FaFaMo	1		3.2		
MoMoMo	1		.2		
FaFaMoMo	2		1.0		
FaFaFaMo	2		.5		
FaFaFaFaMo	1		.6		
MoFaFaFaMo	1		.6		
All	19	24.0	11.8	12.6	.66
Non-cognates	2	2.5	.9	1.0	.45
Total non-residents	24	30.5	16.7	17.9	.70
Grand total all members	79	100.0	93.3	100.0	1.18

* All non-agnatic cognates are classified by kinship link to the agnatic ancestors of the parish.

APPENDIX III

Extent of Land-Holding and Parish Membership

Categories compared	Men	Acres	Acreage per man	Level of significance*
Resident members	55	76.6	1.39	Not
Non-resident members	24	16.7	1.18	
Agnatic members	23	44.7	1.94	+
Non-agnatic cognatic members	50	46.9	.94	
Agnatic residents	20	40.7	2.03	Not
Agnatic non-residents	3	4	1.33	
Agnatic unilocal residents	8	22.7	2.84	Not
Agnatic multilocal residents	12	18	1.50	
Non-agnatic cognatic residents	31	31.1	1.0	Not
Non-agnatic cognatic non-residents	19	11.8	.66	
Non-agnatic cognatic unilocal residents	7	5.6	.8	Not
Non-agnatic cognatic multilocal residents	24	29.5	1.23	
Unilocal residents	17	28.7	1.69	Not
Multilocal residents	38	47.9	1.23	
Unilocal agnatic residents	8	22.7	2.84	Not
Unilocal non-agnatic cognatic residents	7	5.6	.80	
Multilocal agnatic residents	12	18	1.5	Not
Multilocal non-agnatic cognatic residents	24	29.5	1.23	
Non-resident agnates	3	4	1.33	Not
Non-resident non-agnatic cognates	19	11.8	.66	
Patrilateral members	52	73	1.40	Not
Matrilateral members	27	20.3	.75	
Agnatic members	23	44.7	1.94	Not
Other patrilateral members	29	28.3	.98	

APPENDIX III. *Continued*

Other patrilateral members	29	28.3	.98 ⎫	Not
Matrilateral members	27	20.3	.75 ⎭	
Agnatic members	23	44.7	1.94 ⎫	++
Matrilateral members	27	20.3	.75 ⎭	

* Levels of statistical significance:
+ 5 per cent level.
++ 2 per cent level.

APPENDIX IV

Huli Kin Terms

Cognatic:

hamene (m)*	Brothers; seminal and uterine half-brothers; all parallel cousins.
hagapuni (f)*	Sister; seminal and uterine half-sisters; all parallel cousins.
*mbalini**	Sibling of opposite sex; same range of extension as 1 and 2.
*hamini**	Cross-cousin of either sex.
apa	Fathers; father's brother; all relatives father calls brother.
ainyia	Mother: mother's sister; all relatives mother calls sister.
*adyena**	Father's brother.
*apapuni**	Mother's brother.
*arapuni**	Father's sister.
*amma**	Mother's sister.
*mama**	Grandfather; grandfather's brothers.
*iaya** (or *agua*)	Grandmother; grandmother's sisters.
igini	Son; brother's son.
wane	Daughter; brother's daughter.
*mamavuni**	Child of a cross-cousin.
apa (yamuwini)	a. A parent's cross-cousin's child. b. A grandparent's cross-cousin's grandchild. c. Any descendants of the same generation from cross-sex siblings.

Affinal kin terms:

one	Wife.
agalini	Husband.
*hagarini**	Co-wife.
*kyane**	Husband's brother or male parallel cousin.
*aruni**	a. Husband's sister or female parallel cousin. b. All husband's relatives other than *kyane*.
*imane**	Wife's parents, aunts, uncles and cross-cousins of any degree.

APPENDICES

Appendix IV. *Continued*

balibuni*	Wife's sibling or parallel cousin of either sex.
yagini*	a. Mother's sister's husband.
	b. Father's co-wife's former husband.

(m) = Male speaking.
(f) = Female speaking.
* = Reciprocal term.
All terms may be used for reference or address.

APPENDIX V

Relationship between Mode of Residence and Age of Huli Men

Age	Unilocal residents	Multilocal residents	Total residents
20-25	21	20	41
26-35	55	73	128
36-45	34	48	82
46-55	27	27	54
56 +	11	5	16
Total	148	173	321
Per cent	46.1	53.9	100

The test shows that age is not directly associated with mode of residence. By regrouping the data, it can be used to determine whether middle-aged men are more likely to be multilocal residents than young and old men. (Middle-age is considered to be 26-45.) The result of this calculation is also negative, and it is safe to infer that age is not associated with mode of residence (chi squared = 3.41, df = 1, $p > .05$).

Relationship between Marital Status and Residence Type of Huli Men

Type of residence	Single	Monogynists	Polygynists	Total	Per cent
Unilocal	27	65	35	127	45.2
Multilocal	16	97	41	154	54.8
Total	43	162	76	281	100.0
Per cent	15.8	57.7	26.5	100	

Chi squared = 3.01, df = 2, $p > .05$.

The result is again negative; there is no significant association between a man's marital status and his mode of residence.

APPENDIX VI

A Bride Price Conflict

Ligia's seduction of Wandume had consequences apart from those already discussed. Yagari, her father's brother, set off another train of events when he distributed Wandume's first bride price, which had been paid by Belopo. The payment comprised 15 pigs, including 4 large sows. Because Wandume's liaison with Ligia had precipitated a war involving his parish-section (Kore-*Kimabe*) in various claims, Yagari sent only one sow to her mother's brother as the maternal portion, instead of the conventional 5 pigs. Yagari regarded Wandume as the initiator of his troubles and felt justified in using most of her bride price to pay reparations. Wandume's maternal kin, however, did not agree with this arrangement, but at the time they were unable to contest it.

Several months later, before the marriage was consummated, Belolo was killed, and Wandume returned to Kore-*Kimabe* territory. As the marriage was of brief duration, Bepolo's brothers asked for the return of the full bride price. Yagari sent back three of the original pigs but, as he could not then recover the rest, promised to return equivalent pigs when Wandume re-married. One pig he returned was that which he had originally given to Wandume's mother's brother.

Wandume next married Tebela of Kore-*Liapo*. (Neither Wandume nor Tebela was a Kore agnate.) Tebela gave a bride price of 15 pigs, of which 4 were sows. Yagari distributed the pigs, giving Bepolo's brothers 9 (including 2 sows) to their satisfaction. He kept one sow as his share and gave one barrow to a Kore-*Wipo* man, who had previously contributed to a Kore-*Kimabe* reparation. Yagari also gave one small pig to Igibe, Wandume's father's sister's son (who had previously received a sow which was later returned to Bepolo). Igibe refused the pig, saying that it was too small, and in its place seized the fourth sow and its two sucklings which Yagari intended for Goya, Wandume's mother's brother. The pig which Igibe refused was taken by Wandume on behalf of her mother.

The pig intended for Wandume's mother, however, was not actually given to her. Instead, Wandume's husband, Tebela, reared it to maturity and exchanged it for another. At this time Tebela worked for the Administration on road construction and was often away from Kore-territory. Without consulting him, Wandume, who had been living alone, went to live in a women's house with the wife of Perege of Kore-*Kimabe*, a man who had been her guardian after her father's death. Perege had not received any portion of Wandume's bride price, however, and one day when Tebela came to see her, Wandume urged him to give Perege a pig. The suggestion annoyed Tebela, who not only berated Wandume for living in Perege's house, but also accused her of committing adultery with Perege.

When Perege heard of the accusation he demanded compensation from Tebela for impugning his name. As Tebela had few close kinsmen and Perege had many, Tebela swallowed his pride and handed over a pig.

Despite the birth of a son to Tebela, his marriage with Wandume ended in divorce after two years. Wandume left Tebela and returned with the child to Kore-*Kimabe*. Her father's brother, Yagari, promised to return Tebela's bride price when she remarried.

Wandume's third husband, Munumbu, paid 15 pigs (including 3 sows) to Yagari in bride price. When they were delivered, however, Handobe, a bigman of Agona, intervened and claimed 3 pigs for Agona-*Eyagu*, Wandume's mother's (agnatic) section, which so far had received no part of her bride prices. A heated argument developed among the claimants for Munumbu's bride price. Tebela asserted that a return payment of 12 pigs (including 2 sows) was an inadequate return, because Wandume had not only left him but had also taken his infant son. Agona-*Eyagu* men asserted that they were entitled to a share as Wandume's maternal kin. After a long and acrimonious debate, Tebela and Wandume's paternal and maternal kin all agreed that Igibe, who had received the sow and three sucklings originally intended for Agona-*Eyagu*, should pay one sow in compensation to Tebela. Tebela was then willing to accept the 12 pigs from Munumbu's bride price. Nevertheless, men not directly concerned in the matter said that Tebela should have given up two pigs of his bride price, because his son by Wandume would in fact return to him when old enough to leave the mother.

The earlier grievance between Tebela and Perege was also discussed publicly, but nothing more was done about it. A distant kinsman of both men suggested that, as they were both men of Kore, they should settle the issue amicably. To this Perege retorted that a marriage had occurred between agnates of *Kimabe* and *Liapo*, and therefore, they were no longer kin.

This history is typical of Huli bride price disputes. It shows the ramifications of a simple event—of the failure of a girl's guardian to distribute her bride price according to convention. The dispute did not lead to warfare mainly because the injured men lived too far away to defend their rights at the time. However, they did not forget the injustice and at the distribution of the girl's third bride price, they successfully pressed their claim.

BIBLIOGRAPHY

AITCHISON, T. G.
    1936   "Peace Ceremony as Performed by the Natives of the Ramu Headwaters", *Oceania*, 6:478-81.

BARNES, J. A.
    1949   "Measures of Divorce Frequency in Simple Societies", *Journal of the Royal Anthropological Institute*, 79:37-62.

BARRAU, J.
    1958   "Subsistence Agriculture in Melanesia", *Bishop Museum Bulletin*, 219.

BERNDT, R. M.
    1955   "Interdependence and Conflict in the Eastern Highlands of New Guinea", *Man*, 55, No. 116.

BROWN, P. and BROOKFIELD, H.
    1959   "Chimbu Land and Society", *Oceania*, 30:1-75

BUREAU FOR NATIVE AFFAIRS, Netherlands New Guinea
    1958   "Anthropological Research in Netherlands New Guinea since 1950", *Oceania*, Monograph No. 10.

COLSON, E.
    1953   "Social Control and Vengeance in Plateau Tonga Society", *Africa*, 23:199-212.

DAVENPORT, WILLIAM
    1959   "Nonunilinear Descent and Descent Groups", *American Anthropologist*, 61:557-572.

EMBER, MELVIN
    1959   "The Nonunilinear Descent Groups of Samoa", *American Anthropologist*, 61:573-577.

FORTES, MEYER
    1953   "The Structure of Unilineal Descent Groups", *American Anthropologist*, 55:17-41.
    1959   "Descent, Filiation and Affinity: A rejoinder to Dr. Leach", part II, *Man*, 59, No. 331.

FORTUNE, R. F.
- 1947 "The Rules of Relationship Behaviour in one Variety of Primitive Warfare", *Man*, 47, No. 115.
- 1947 "Law and Force in Papuan Societies", *American Anthropologist*, 49:244-259.

FREEMAN, J. D.
- 1960 *The Iban of Western Borneo, in Social Structure in Southeast Asia*, G. P. Murdock (ed.), New York.

GOODENOUGH, W. H.
- 1951 "Property, Kin and Community on Truk", *Yale University Publications in Anthropology*, 46.
- 1955 "A Problem in Malayo-Polynesian Social Organisation", *American Anthropologist*, 57:71-83.

GRAY, ROBERT F.
- 1960 "Sonjo Bride Price and the Question of African 'Wife Purchase' ", *American Anthropologist*, 62:34-57.

GROVES, W. C.
- 1935 "Natives of Sio Island", *Oceania*, 5:43-63.

HIDES, J.
- 1936 *Papuan Wonderland*, London.

HOCART, A. M.
- 1931 "Warfare in Eddystone of the Solomons", *Journal of the Royal Anthropological Institute*, 61:301-324.

HOEBEL, E. ADAMSON
- 1954 *The Law of Primitive Man*, Harvard University Press, Cambridge.

HOGBIN, H. I.
- 1939 *Experiments in Civilization*, London.

HOGBIN, H. I. and WEDGWOOD, CAMILLA H.
- 1953 "Local Grouping in Melanesia", *Oceania*, 23:4; 24:58-76.

HUBER, HUGO.
- 1959 "Ritual Oaths as Instruments of Coercion and Self Defence among the Adamne of Ghana", *Africa*, 29:41-49.

KIRCHOFF, PAUL
- 1955 "The Principles of Clanship in Human Society", *Davidson Journal of Anthropology*, 1:1-10.

LANCASTER, LORRAINE
- 1958 "Kinship in Anglo-Saxon Society", *British Journal of Sociology*, 9:230-250; 359-377.

LEACH, E. R.
- 1948 "Some Features of Social Structure Among Sarawak Pagans", *Man*, 54, No. 103.
- 1950 "Social Science Research in Sarawak", *Colonial Research Study*, 1:61, 72.

1960 "The Sinhalese of the Dry Zone of Northern Ceylon", in *Social Structure in Southeast Asia*, G. P. Murdock (ed.), New York.
1961 *Pul Eliya—A Village in Ceylon—A Study of Land Tenure and Kinship*, Cambridge.

MEGGITT, M. J.
1956 "The Valleys of the Upper Wage and Lai Rivers", *Oceania*, 27:90-135.
1957a "Mae Enga Political Organization", *Mankind*, 4:133-137.
1957b "The Ipili of the Porgera Valley, Western Highlands District, Territory Papua New Guinea", *Oceania*, 28:31-55.
1958 "The Enga of the New Guinea Highlands: Some Preliminary Observations", *Oceania*, 28:253-330.
1959 *The Lineage System of the Mae Enga of New Guinea*. Unpublished Ph.D. thesis, Sydney University.

MURDOCK, G. P. (ed.)
1960 *Social Structure in Southeast Asia*, Viking Fund Publication, No. 29, "Cognatic Forms of Social Organization".

MURPHY, ROBERT F.
1957 "Intergroup Hostility and Social Cohesion", *American Anthropologist*, 59:1018-1035.

PETERS, EMRYS
1960 "The Proliferation of Lineage Segments in Cyrenaica", *Journal of the Royal Anthropological Institute*, 90:29-53.

POSPISIL, LEOPOLD
1958 "Kapauku Papuans and Their Law", *Yale University Publications in Anthropology*, No. 54.

POUWER, J.
1960 "Loosely Structured Societies in Netherlands New Guinea", *Bijdragen Taal-, Land- en Volkenkunde*, 116:109-118.
1960 "Social Structure in the Western Interior of Sarmi (Northern Netherlands New Guinea), A Response to a Response", *Bijdragen Taal-, Land- en Volkenkunde*, 116:363-372.

RADCLIFFE-BROWN, A. R. and FORDE, DARYLL (ed.)
1950 *African Systems of Kinship and Marriage*, London.

READ, K. E.
1959 "Leadership and Consensus in a New Guinea Society", *American Anthropologist*, 61:425-66.

REAY, MARIE
1959 *The Kuma*, Melbourne.
1959 "Two Kinds of Ritual Conflict", *Oceania*, 29:290-296.

RIVERS, W. H. R.
1924 *Social Organisation*, London.

RYAN D'ARCY
1955 "Clan Organisation in the Mendi Valley, Southern Highlands of Papua New Guinea", *Oceania*, 26:79-90.
1959 "Clan Formation in the Mendi Valley", *Oceania*, 29:257-289.

SAHLINS, MARSHALL D.
- 1961 "The Segmentary Lineage: An Organisation of Predatory Expansion", *American Anthropologist*, 63:322-345.

SCHAPERA, I.
- 1955 "The Sin of Cain", *Journal of the Royal Anthropological Institute*, 85:31-43.

SINCLAIR, J. P.
- 1958a "The Duna People of the Papuan Highlands", *Walkabout*, 32-37.
- 1958b "The Duna People of the Papuan Highlands", *Walkabout*, 30-32.

SOLIAN, NANCIE L.
- 1959 "The Nonunilineal Descent Group in the Caribbean and Central America", *American Anthropologist*, 61:578-583.

TODD, J. A.
- 1934 "Report on Research Work in South-West New Britain, Territory of New Guinea", *Oceania*, 5:80-101; 193-312.
- 1935 "Native Offences and European Law in South-West New Britain"' *Oceania*, 5:437-460.
- 1936 "Redress of Wrongs in South-West New Britain", *Oceania*, 6:401-440.

VAN DER LEEDEN, A. C.
- 1960 "Social Structure in New Guinea", *Bijdragen, Taal-, Land- en Volkenkunde*, 116:119-149.

WEDGWOOD, CAMILLA H.
- 1930 "Some Aspects of Warfare in Melanesia", *Oceania*, 1:3-31.

WEST, F. J.
- 1956 "Colonial Development in the Central New Guinea Highlands", *Pacific Affairs*, 29:161-173.

WHITE, LESLIE A.
- 1959 *The Evolution of Culture*, New York.

WILLIAMS, F. E.
- 1931 "Sex Affiliation and its Implications", *Journal of the Royal Anthropological Institute*, 61:51-82.
- 1938 *Report on the Grasslanders, Augu, Woge and Wela. Appendix to the Report of the Administration of the Territory of Papua.*
- 1941 "Group Sentiment and Primitive Justice", *American Anthropologist*, 43:523-539.
- 1941 *Natives of Lake Kutubu, Papua, Oceania*, Monograph No. 6.

WURM, S. A.
- 1961 "The Languages of the Eastern, Western and Southern Highlands, T.P.N.G.", in *Linguistic Survey of the South-Western Pacific*, A. Capell (ed.), South Pacific Commission, Noumea.

IMPRIMERIE NATIONALE
7 565 036 6